UNDERSTANDING THE
ORIGIN & EVOLUTION
OF
SPORT

UNDERSTANDING THE ORIGIN & EVOLUTION OF SPORT

Volume 1

RUGBY UNION

Dai Richards

Dai Richards

Limited Edition

Number 108 *of 2500*

www.rugbyrelics.com

Shy Fly Grin Win

For my wife Hayley

and my children

Laurie, Victoria, Dale & Simon

Published in the United Kingdom by

Rugby Relics Ltd
66 Brynhyfrd
Glynneath
Neath
SA11 5BA
UK

www.rugbyrelics.com

First published 2016

British Library Cataloguing-in-Publication data
A catalogue record for this book is available from the British Library.

ISBN 978-0-9531714-1-5

Updates and further information relating to this title will be published on the following websites

www.world-rugby-museum.com

www.origin-of-sport.com

CONTENTS

SOURCES OF REFERENCE MATERIAL

AAME – 'MEMORIES OF ETON' by Arthur Campbell Ainger, published by John Murray, London, 1917

APRL – 'HISTORY OF THE LAWS OF RUGBY FOOTBALL' by Admiral Sir Percy Royds, 1948

CAFA – 1883 FOOTBALL ANNUAL edited by Charles Alcock, published by The Cricket Press

CALT – 'MY LIFE AND TIMES' by Nimrod (Charles Apperley), edited with additions by E. D. Cuming, published by William Blackwood and Sons Limited, London & Edinburgh, 1927

CRSO – 'THE SHARED ORIGINS OF FOOTBALL, RUGBY AND SOCCER' by Christopher Rowley, published by Rowman & Littlefied, 2015 – ISBN 9781442246188

FMRU – 'FOOTBALL – THE RUGBY UNION GAME' by Reverend Frank Marshall (2nd edition), 1894

FMWW – 'WEBB ELLIS – 'FICTION OR FACTS' by Floris van der Merwe, 1999 – ISBN 0620248513

FORU – Football Rules – Rugby School 1845 – facsimile edition published by Rugby School, 2015

HCBR – 'RUGBY' – by H.C. Brady B.A., published by George Bell and Sons, London, 1900

HRGH – 'A GAME FOR HOOLIGANS – THE HISTORY OF RUGBY UNION' by Huw Richards, published by Mainstream, 2006 – ISBN 1845960165

JGPR – 'THE PHOENIX BOOK OF INTERNATIONAL RUGBY RECORDS' by John Griffiths, published by JM Dent & Sons Ltd, London, 1987 – ISBN 0460070037

JMRB – 1991 – 'RUNNING WITH THE BALL – THE BIRTH OF RUGBY FOOTBALL' by Jenny Macrory, published by Collins Willow, 1991 – ISBN 0002184028

JRWR – 'THE WORLD OF RUGBY' by John Reason & Carwyn James, published by the BBC, 1979 – ISBN 0563162805

LCFG – 'THE FIELD GAME' by Lachlan Campbell published by Essential Works Limited, 2013 – ISBN 9781906615802

LEVS = LONDON EVENING STANDARD – Daily newspaper

METR – THE METEOR – Rugby School Publication

MBRN – 'RUGBY– THE SCHOOL AND NEIGHBOURHOOD' collected and arranged from the writings of the late Matthew Holbeche Bloxam, O.R., F.S.A., by the Rev. W.H. Payne Smith M.A., published by Whittaker & Co, London, 1889

MLHE – 'A HISTORY OF ETON COLLEGE' Sir H.C. Maxwell-Lyte, K.C.B., 1911 edition

MRFP – 'MACREADY'S REMINISCENCES AND SELECTIONS FROM HIS DIARIES AND LETTERS' by Sir Frederick Pollock, Bart (one of his executors), published by MacMillan and Co, 1875

MSAF – 'ATHLETICS & FOOTBALL' by Montague Shearman, published by Longmans Green & Co, London, part of the Badminton Library Series, 1887

MSFC – 'FOOTBALL – ITS HISTORY FOR FIVE CENTURIES' by Montague Shearman & James E. Vincent, published by Field & Tuer, 1885

MSFT – 'FOOTBALL' by Montague Shearman, published by Longmans Green & Co, London, part of the Badminton Library Series, 1899

NHSR – NATURAL HISTORY SOCIETY REPORT – Rugby School publication

OPED – OXFORD POPULAR ENGLISH DICTIONARY, 2000 edition

ORSR – 'THE ORIGIN OF RUGBY FOOTBALL', report (with appendices) of the sub-committee of the Old Rugbeian Society appointed in July 1895, 1897

PTRF – 'RUGBY UNION FOOTBALL' by Captain Philip Trevor "Dux", 1903

RHBF – 'ROUTLEDGE'S HANDBOOK OF FOOTBALL', published by George Routledge and Sons, 1867

RMOU – 'CENTENARY HISTORY – OXFORD UNIVERSITY RUGBY FOOTBALL CLUB 1869–1969' by Ross McWhirter & Sir Andrew Noble, 1969

RMPW – 'POSITIONS WHEREIN THOSE PRIMITATIVE CIRCUMSTANCES BE EXAMINED, WHICH ARE NECESSARIE FOR THE TRAINING UP OF CHILDREN' by Richard Mulcaster, 1581

RSRE – Rugby School Register, various dates

SSUG – 'THE UNION GAME – A RUGBY HISTORY' by Sean Smith, published by BBC Worldwide, 1999 – ISBN 0563551186

TCOW – 'THE OVAL WORLD – A GLOBAL HISTORY OF RUGBY' by Tony Collins, 2015 – ISBN 9781408843703

WRHR – 'A HISTORY OF RUGBY' by Wallace Reyburn, published by Arthur Baker Ltd, London, 1971 – ISBN 0213004860

WRRS – 'HISTORY OF RUGBY SCHOOL' by W.H.D. Rouse M.A., published by Duckworth & Co, London, 1898

WRUH – 1978–79 WELSH RUGBY UNION HANDBOOK

CHAPTER 1 – THE BEGINNING

Hello, how do you do? My name is David, my kids call me Dad, my Mrs and close friends call me Dave, in the local swimming pool they call me Dai Splash and when I'm doing karaoke I'm called Shy Dai. Lyn Jones the rugby coach calls me Dai Rucksack and I'm known as Dai 'something or other' in several other places. That's just the way things are in Wales, most of us are called David, or Dai for short, followed by our occupations – 'Dai the Milk', 'Dai Barber', 'Dai Banknote' (the accountant) – or followed by a trait – 'Dai Bungalow' (nothing upstairs), 'Dai Cakey' (likes cakes), 'Dai Bend the Truth' (tells lies), Dai Tra La La (member of four choirs) etc. This book is about a journey I've recently undertaken. About how I learnt to understand the origin of the sport of Rugby Union, and there was a point on this journey where I was the only person alive with this knowledge. But I don't want to be known as 'Dai Lonely Origin', so I'd like to share this information with you. Please join me in my journey of understanding as I tell it like my singing buddies Frank Sinatra & Sid Vicious .... 'My Way'

The journey began at the dentist, halfway between the hygienist and my check up with the main man Matthew White – he once met Roald Dahl you know – but that's his story, back to mine. My phone rang and I didn't have my glasses on, so I pressed the wrong button and cancelled the call. The call was from an auction house in London where a William Webb Ellis signed letter dated 1826 was up for auction. I had booked a telephone line to place my bid and I'd just cut the auctioneers off. I panicked, I was going to miss my opportunity to bid. I rang the auction house but only got through to reception. Plan B was that the auction house would ring my office number, and luckily my wife Hayley knows how to press the right buttons and say the right words, so she bought the Webb Ellis letter.

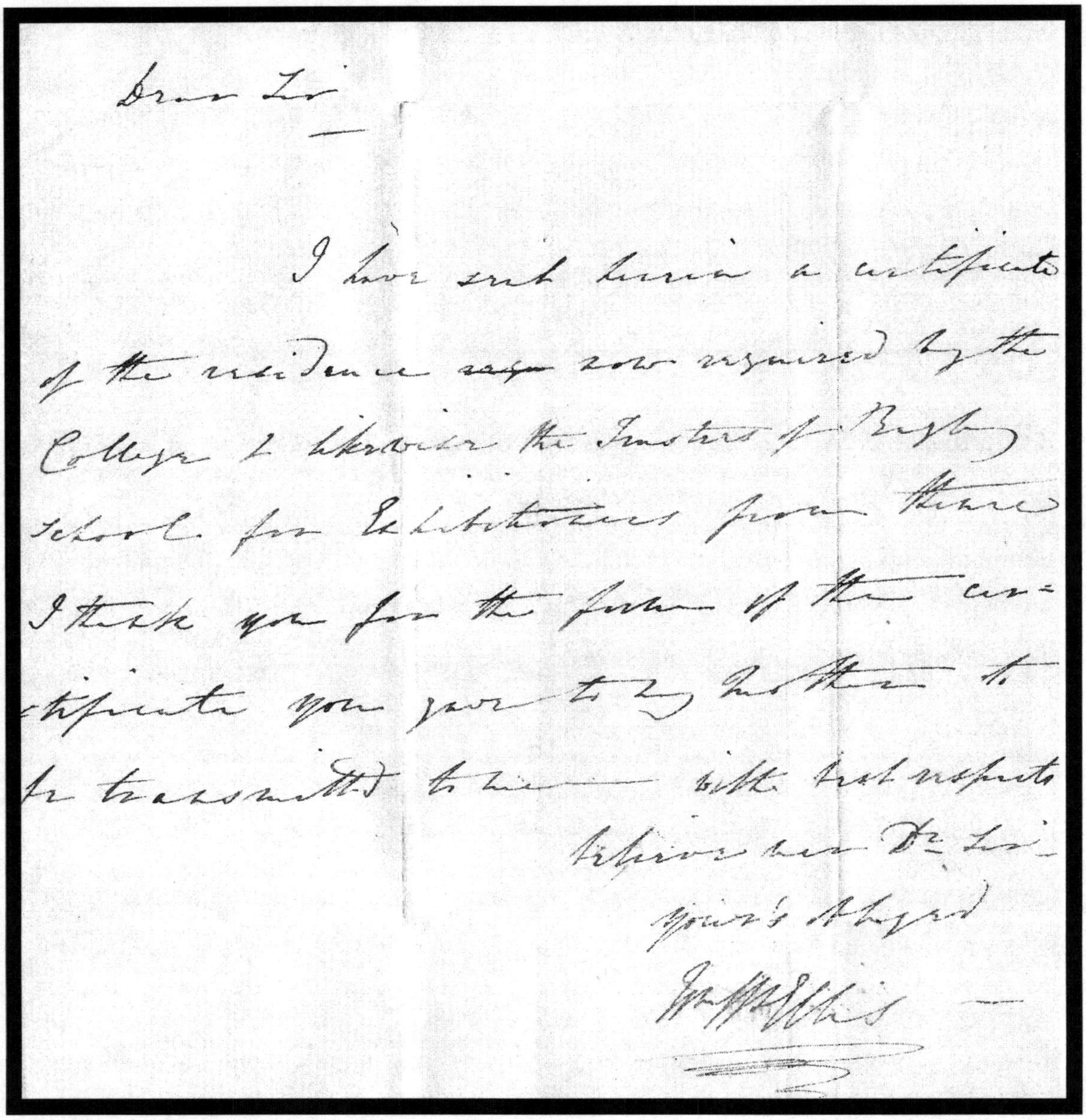

Dear Sir

I have sent herein a certificate of the residence now required by the College & likewise the masters (?) of Rugby School for Exhibitioners from there. I thank you for the ??? of the cer - tificate you gave my mother to be transmitted to her (?) with best respects

???? ???? Dr Sir

yours obliged

W W Ellis

Why did I buy a William Webb Ellis letter? I started collecting rugby memorabilia in 1968, I was only 8 years old at the time, just a lad, and I continued collecting rugby things as a child, building a collection that focused on my favourite club, Neath, and my country, Wales. I started working in 1978 and also started buying memorabilia from dealers. Sometimes the things I wanted from the dealers had already been sold when I went to buy them, so I thought to myself 'how can I get these things before the dealers do?' I started wheeling and dealing myself to improve my collection and I was good at it, so in 1991 I started Rugby Relics – a business that focused entirely on selling rugby memorabilia. The collection improved and to showcase it ten years later I opened the world's first on-line rugby museum www.world-rugby-museum.com. Since then I have displayed some of my collection at the Welsh Rugby Union's 125th anniversary exhibition and at their 130th anniversary dinner, but I always struggled to show something that linked in with the development of the sport at Rugby School. With my Webb Ellis signature in hand I now had the means to do this, with what I believed at the time to be the oldest existing item of rugby memorabilia.

I've always been intrigued by the William Webb Ellis story. I've read several books and articles that have written the story off as myth and, as a rule, I tended to agree with these theories without questioning them. So I set out to learn about the Webb Ellis story and how he was supposed to have invented the sport of Rugby Union. I only intended to write a short article, it was just going to be a page on the website, but the more I delved into the origin of rugby, the more I wrote about it and the more I realised that there was a general lack of understanding about the origin of Rugby Union and about the origin of a sport in general. Then my article became too long for a single webpage and 'writing a book' was on my bucket list, so here we are today. It's a happy first book for 'Dai Author' or 'Dai Origin' as I might become known in the future.

I would like you to join me in analysing the origin of the sport of Rugby Union, so from here on in every so often I'm going to use 'we' and 'us', and when I say 'we' or 'us', I mean you, the person who is reading the book and me, the one who has written it.

At the beginning of every chapter I'm going to let you know what the aim of that chapter is, but first here is the aim of this book.

AIM – To understand the origin of the sport of Rugby Union.

At the end of every chapter I'm going to give you a

SUMMARY – On what we've talked about in the chapter and a

CONCLUSION – On what we've decided

This may be followed by a

FOOTNOTE – A note that is at the foot of each chapter. Everyone is different, I have my own style of writing, which you may or may not enjoy. The topics I'm covering in this book are quite serious so I've tried a Jekyll & Hyde approach to the book. I hope it's a good analogy because I haven't read that book. Within the chapters themselves I'm trying to be Dr Jekyll, seriously analysing the origin of Rugby Union. But in the footnotes I let loose with my own personality. I'm not so much of a Mr Hyde, more of a Mr Silly, but if this is to be my only book I want it to reflect some of my eccentricities. Think of it this way: put yourself in the shoes of a top Association football player (a footballer, a soccer player, whatever you want to call him or her) playing in a cup final. You've just spent 90 minutes focusing entirely on one thing, on winning a game of soccer, and you've pushed yourself to the limits of physical exertion. You've just scored a goal, it was the winning goal and it was in the last minute. You have to celebrate, run around and do silly dances, because that's what soccer players do. This book is my cup final, I'm Welsh and I'm a Welsh sportsman who as a rule doesn't write books, so when I finish a chapter I'm going to celebrate and I'm going to sing in celebration, because that's what Welshmen do when they are happy. We sing. This is a bit difficult on paper but you'll get the gist of it as we go along. You may or may not enjoy my style of writing and so to help you decide on the best way in which way to approach this book, here are four options on how you can get the most out of it:

1. I'M IN A RUSH – If you are in a hurry, turn straight to the conclusion in Chapter 11 to read about how the game of Rugby Union began, close the book and have a nice day.

2. I'M TOO SERIOUS TO READ YOUR BOOK – Although I love to have fun and chat a little, I'm serious about sport and once you get into the book you'll find it very informative and downright serious. I also hope to write a follow up book focusing entirely on the origin of Rugby Union so you may wish to wait for that.

3. I'M NEAT AND TIDY AND DON'T WANT TO MARK THE BOOK – There are a few options for adding photos in the book, for writing information about yourself and participating in the study of a sport; you don't have to do this if you don't want to. Some people just don't mark books and if you are one of those people then that's fine.

4. I WANT TO JOIN YOU ON YOUR JOURNEY OF DISCOVERY – Great stuff, glad you're on board, let's go...............

So that you can put a face to the words, here are three photos of myself.

Left: This is me with the Rugby World Cup and the Webb Ellis letter.
Centre: This is me after I shaved my head in 1983 to teach myself a lesson.
Right: This is me being chased by Ghurkas, Paratroopers and the SAS over the mountains of North Wales.

But enough about me, what about you? Please write your name below

I am ....

And add some pictures of yourself in whatever pose you want.

REFERENCES & SOURCE INFORMATION

I don't have an academic background, I left school with two 'O' levels (GCSEs), and when I started the book I didn't know how to do those little numbers in the text for sources that historians use. I don't like them anyway because every time I'd turn to find out where a source's information had come from I'd lose my place, so I've invented my own reference system based on what I would prefer when reading a book or other publication.

BOOKS - I've used a 7 figure code for each reference or source of information obtained from books and this code can be found next to the information. The first 4 letters refer to a publication and the 3 numbers that follow refer to a page number in that publication.

For example: ORSR011 = Old Rugbeian Society Report page 11

The exception to this rule is if the page is part of a preface or introduction then the page number will be shown as 0 followed by additional information that will help to identify that page, e.g. 0pf2 is preface page 2. If the reference is spread over two or more pages then it's the page on which the reference starts that is used.

NEWSPAPERS – For newspaper sources I've used a 4 letter code to identify the newspaper and followed it with the date of publication in an 8 figure format.

For example: LEVS18721023 = London Evening Standard 1872 – 10 (October) - 23

If you wish to view the actual sources and references used in the book, these can all be found on www.world-rugby-museum.com – just go to the home page and click on ORIGIN SOURCES directly below the rugby ball image. You'll find a list of the publications with their codes earlier in the book but if you do want to check out the sources (and you have an internet device close to hand) you can do so while you are reading the book. You'll also find many reference materials in the book and occasionally these are repeated because I would like you to digest the information as you read it again. This book is about understanding and sometimes you may need to read a chapter again to comprehend the points made. This is a complicated subject and everything we've been told about the origin of Rugby Union over the last 100 plus years is nonsense, so clear your mind and let's start again. If you haven't got the time, take the number one option on how to get the best out of this book and move on.

TERMINOLOGY

The term 'football' has a different meaning nowadays than it had in the early days of the development of Rugby Union, so for the purpose of clarification we will use the following terminology wherever possible for the various forms of football and other related subject matter used in this book.

FOOTBALL – This was a term used for anything that related to kicking or handling a ball prior to the formation of The Football Association in 1863.

FOLK FOOTBALL – Ancient forms of football described in various publications, such as harpastum, Ball of Scone, Corfe Castle, Derby football, etc. This is also sometimes referred to as 'mob football'.

FOOTBALL AT RUGBY SCHOOL – Football as played at Rugby School up until the first rules were written in 1845. This is universally recognised by all as the early developmental stage of Rugby Union. This is the game that William Webb Ellis played.

RUGBY SCHOOL RULES – Football as played under the Rules of Rugby School. This is after the first set of rules was published in 1845 and before the Rugby Football Union was founded in 1871. This is the secondary developmental stage of Rugby Union and links Football at Rugby School to Rugby Union. Former pupils of Rugby School took their printed football rule book to the universities, clubs and other schools where they played football under the rules of Rugby School.

RUGBY UNION FOOTBALL OR RUGBY UNION – The sport of Rugby Union as administered initially by the Rugby Football Union in 1871 and as is now administered by World Rugby in 2016.

WILLIAM WEBB ELLIS EVENT – The moment when it is said that William Webb Ellis caught the ball and ran forward with it, sometime between 1823 and 1825.

EARLIEST AGREED POINT OF ORIGIN – The earliest point in time where it is agreed by all acceptable theorists (see Chapter 14) that a game or a sport exists. In the case of Rugby Union this is 1823–1825 at the William Webb Ellis event. This does not mean that everyone believes that William Webb Ellis invented the game. It just means that everyone agrees that the game that was being played directly after the Webb Ellis event at Rugby School is the one that is today known as Rugby Union. There are no arguments as to the development of the sport of Rugby Union from this date onwards. Everyone agrees that the game of Football that was being played at Rugby School in 1826 is the same game that has developed into the sport of Rugby Union that is being played under the rules of 'World Rugby' today.

FOOTNOTE – OK let's move on. Firstly we need to see how the history of Rugby Union has been recorded throughout the years. That should give us a good indication of where to start looking for the origin of Rugby Union. Before we do move on, here's a gentle warm up for the footnotes of future chapters..............

"The road is long,
There are mountains in our way"......

Joe Cocker – "Up Where We Belong" – 1990

......Climb every mountain
Ford every stream
Follow every rainbow
'Till you find your dream

Rodgers & Hammerstein – "Sound of Music" – 1965

CHAPTER 2 – RECORDING THE HISTORY OF RUGBY FOOTBALL

AIM – To look at how the history of rugby football has been recorded since the earliest publications which cover football to modern day publications dedicated to the history of Rugby Union.

1867 – ROUTLEDGE'S HANDBOOK OF FOOTBALL

The first recorded history of football is in a book published by George Routledge & Sons in 1867 – 'Routledge's Handbook of Football'. The book covers information relating to football in general, including styles of play, costume and laws. It focuses mainly on the public school games, championing in particular football as played at Rugby School. It's worth quoting this lengthy passage from the chapter 'How the Game is Played' because it gives a good overview of football in England. It also highlights what the 'ball in hand' crowd thought of the 'ball at feet' crowd:

"It would be devoting more space, than I have at present at command, to give – much as I should have liked to have done so – the rules of every school and every club in England where football is played. I am sure they would have been found almost in every instance dissimilar. I have contented myself therefore with selecting good examples of rules used in schools; (1), those which maintain that running and handling the ball is a heresy, and (2) those which maintain an exactly contrary opinion. Here of course is the great bone of contention. The principal schools which hold the first opinion, are of course Eton, Harrow, Westminster, Charterhouse, and the majority of the older schools; while the more modern ones, headed by Rugby, which has brought the game, in my opinion, to the perfection of a science, maintain the latter. To the two sections of rules to which I have alluded, I have added the rules drawn out by the Football Association, a band of antagonistic brethren who met together in London and attempted a compromise, but from whose efforts not much good has hitherto sprung. Lovers of Football are the most conservative people in the world, and real lovers of Football are necessarily a little bigoted where reform is concerned." – RHBF022

In the chapter 'The History of the Game', Routledge mentions forms of ancient folk football including 'Derby Football' and the 'Ball of Scone', but is non-committal regarding the origin of football and how it began at the public schools. The chapter begins:

"The same inconsistencies and incongruities which will be found elsewhere in connexion with this game, crop up at the very outset. In almost everything connected with football doctors differ. I shall have to say something eventually about the difference

of opinion which exists with regard to the manner in which the game should be played, and now I find that no one seems to be agreed as to how the game originated." – RHBF012

It is worth noting that Routledge called all games using a round or oval ball 'football'. If the game involved kicking or carrying the ball, then as far as he was concerned it was football. This was the general rule up until this date, but as the popularity of Association football grew, 'football' became the accepted term for that sport.

1885 – FOOTBALL – ITS HISTORY FOR FIVE CENTURIES

The next publication we look at is Montague Shearman and James E Vincent's 'Football – Its History for Five Centuries' published in 1885 by Field & Tuer. In the preface, Shearman & Vincent state:

"There also resulted a theory, which was not adopted without anxious argument, that the games of football now in vogue owe their origin almost entirely to the public schools; and that in the public schools rules were the consequence of circumstances and environment. At the same time football has a history which has been faithfully followed." – MSFC0pf.v

Shearman and Vincent state that there is one exception to the above rule – Football at Rugby School, which is the 'original' folk football game that survived only at the school because of its wide open spaces:

"The conditions of football were different at Rugby from those which prevailed at other schools; or rather, to put the matter in language paradoxical in appearance but literally correct, the conditions of the game were normal at Rugby and abnormal everywhere else. In fact, the original form of football,–for it is the simplest,–is of such a nature that it can hardly be played except in a wide open space. Such a space existed at Rugby from the beginning, but not at the other great public schools." – MSFC048

1887 – ATHLETICS & FOOTBALL (subsequent editions: 1888, 1889, & 1894)

Following on from his 1885 book, two years later Shearman published a major work, 'Athletics & Football'. In the chapter on the history of football, he mentions several forms of folk football that have derived from an 'original game'. Again he states that the original game survived and is still being played at Rugby School.

"Probably the name 'football' was first used to describe the ball itself, and meant a ball which was big enough to be kicked and could be kicked with the foot. The game of

football was the game played with this kind of ball, and it was simple to an extreme degree. The goals were two bushes, posts, houses or any objects fixed upon at any distance apart from a few score yards to a few miles. The ball was placed mid-way between the two goals at starting, the players (of any number) divided into two sides, and it was the business of either side to get the ball by force or strategy up to or through the goal of the opposite side. When confined to a street, or field of play, it is obvious that the sport was the original form of what is now known as the Rugby Union game." – MSAF250

1892 – FOOTBALL – THE RUGBY UNION GAME (subsequent editions: 1894 & 1925)

In 1892, the Reverend Frank Marshall published the first in depth history of Rugby Union Football in his book 'Football – The Rugby Union Game'. He quotes extensively from Shearman's 1887 work. He immediately links Rugby Union to folk football:

"Rugby football is the modern scientific development of an ancient game at ball. It can therefore lay claim to be the most ancient of British sports, and in its present form is the legitimate refinement of the rough and crude games which in their main features are undoubtedly the source from which the Rugby game and the Rugby game alone is the true issue." – FMRU001

Later on he pinpoints Shearman's 'original game' as being harpastum as played by the Romans.

"Uniting the extracts, references, and descriptions as above, we can summarise the history of football as played in this island as follows, viz :- That the Romans, who occupied this island during the first four centuries of the Christian era, played at a game of ball called harpastum, which game presented the special features of carrying the ball and the scrummage, found in no other modern game of football save in the Rugby game; that it can be traced back to Roman times that a game of football was played in Britain; and that, as far as can be gathered from tradition, all games then played were characterised by much carrying and little kicking of the ball." – FMRU012

1897 – THE ORIGIN OF RUGBY FOOTBALL

Unhappy with Shearman's claim that Football at Rugby School derived from an 'original' folk football game, The Old Rugbeian Society published a report in 1897 that claimed that the game played in 1823 was like the association game, and that William Webb Ellis was the inventor of rugby football because he broke the rules, caught the ball and ran.

"We now come to Mr. Bloxam's account of the origin of the present Rugby game, which is of such importance that we print it in extenso." – ORSR009

"Ellis, for the first time, disregarded this rule, and on catching the ball, instead of retiring backwards, rushed forwards with the ball in his hands towards the opposite goal..." – ORSR010

1899 – FOOTBALL (subsequent editions: 1901, 1904 & 1908)

The Badminton Library of Athletics and Football was split and re-published as 'Football' only. The chapter on the history of football remains the same but with an addendum in which Montague Shearman concedes that he was wrong about the 'original game' surviving only at Rugby School.

"Since this chapter was written, in 1887, a sub-committee of the Old Rugbeian Society (consisting of Messrs. H. F. Wilson, H.H. Child, A.G. Guillemard, and H.L. Stephen) has paid me the compliment of making a searching investigation, both from historical documents and from inquiry from living Old Rugbeians, with the view to testing my theory that 'at Rugby alone was the old running and collaring game kept up.' The result of their inquiries has been embodied in a pamphlet entitled 'The Origin of Rugby Football,' and published by Mr. Laurence, of Rugby. The writers point out that I was incorrect in my statement that 'Rugby seems to have owned almost from its foundation a wide open grass playground of ample dimensions,' and show that the school had no regular playground until 1749, when it obtained one of 2 a o r. 12 p., and no really 'ample playground' until 1816-17; and the net result of their researches is summed up as follows..." – MSFT034

Shearman then quotes from the Old Rugbeian Society report:

"It may, we think, be fairly considered to be proved from the foregoing statements that (1) in 1820 the form of football in vogue at Rugby was something approximating more closely to Association than what is known as Rugby football to-day; (2) that at some date between 1820 and 1830 the innovation was introduced of running with the ball; (3) that this was in all probability done in the latter half of 1823 by Mr. Webb Ellis . . . To this we would add that the innovation was regarded as of doubtful legality for some time, and only gradually became accepted as part of the game, but obtained a customary status between 1830 and 1840, and was duly legalised first by Bigside Levee in 1841-42 (as stated by Judge Hughes), and finally by the rules of 1846." – MSFT035

Before returning to his declaration of error:

"I think it right to say frankly that the committee (than whom no more competent committee could possibly have been chosen) has, in my view, proved its point, and that the truth appears to be that in the first half of the nineteenth century Rugby school, having then an ample playground, developed a game of football which in its essential features resembled the 'primitive game,' in which every player was allowed to pick up the ball and run with it, and every adversary could stop him by collaring, hacking over, and charging, or any other means he pleased. I can only thank my critics for putting me right upon a matter in which we alike feel a keen interest. – MONATGUE SHEARMAN" – MSFT035

Although Shearman accepts that he was in error about the space available for football at Rugby, he does not mention the Webb Ellis theory himself. He does however quote the above paragraph from the ORS report which mentions Webb Ellis, and Shearman has not challenged this theory. On this basis we must assume that he accepts the Webb Ellis theory as the origin of Rugby Union. With folk football out of the equation, it's left to William Webb Ellis to run forward with the evolutionary ball.

1900 – RUGBY SCHOOL PLAQUE

The William Webb Ellis plaque is cemented into the headmaster's wall at Rugby School.

THIS STONE
COMMEMORATES THE EXPLOIT OF
WILLIAM WEBB ELLIS
WHO WITH A FINE DISREGARD FOR THE RULES OF FOOTBALL
AS PLAYED IN HIS TIME
FIRST TOOK THE BALL IN HIS ARMS AND RAN WITH IT
THUS ORIGINATING THE DISTINCTIVE FEATURE OF
THE RUGBY GAME
A.D. 1823

1903 – RUGBY UNION FOOTBALL

The act of placing the plaque at Rugby School and Shearman's admission of error changed the perceived history of the sport. From then on, the Webb Ellis story was accepted by rugby historians without question and became part of the folklore of Rugby Football. In his book 'Rugby Football', Capt Philip Trevor ("Dux") states in his opening chapter 'Brief General History of Rugby Union Football':

"Rugby Football as a game – that is to say, the practice of picking up the ball and running with it - was due, as most of us know, to the sudden and high handed action of a

little Rugby schoolboy. Then followed the era of big sides when limitless and seething masses of humanity battled for possession of the ball." – PTRF008

1969 – CENTENARY HISTORY – OXFORD UNIVERSITY RUGBY FOOTBALL CLUB

William Webb Ellis entered Oxford University in 1825, just two years after the 'event' on Rugby School Close. Ross McWhirter, co-author of this book on the history of the University, was probably the best authority of his time on William Webb Ellis, and it was he who discovered Ellis' final resting place in Menton, France. McWhirter sits on the fence and states that Ellis was *"such an important name that he demands biographical investigation"* (RMOU012). He then reprints an article titled 'The Rugby Football Mystery', which he wrote for The Times newspaper on 27 Feb 1965. The article starts with the question:

"Was William Ellis really the inventor of Rugby football in November 1823?" – RMOU013

And ends:
"The most certain surmise is that, if this son of a gallant soldier could visit Twickenham for the University match, he would be amazed to see how the pick-up mob football, fifty or so a side (with a pig's bladder) in which he played (and some think cheated at) as a youth, had developed into a sport that is enjoyed by tens of thousands and watched by millions on television in many countries." – RMOU015

The article is very informative, but is non-committal as to whether or not Ellis invented the game.

1971 – A HISTORY OF RUGBY

More doubts about Ellis inventing the game started to appear in print. In his 1971 'A history of Rugby', Wallace Reyburn opens the book with:

"It is a popular misconception that during the course of a soccer match in 1823 a young fellow ran with the ball thus sowing the seed for a handling game which made a radical breakaway from the sport which was literally football. But in fact it was not as clear cut as that. What the Ellis boy did in 1823 at Rugby School was merely to add a new dimension to a handling game already in existence. The match in which the incident took place was certainly not soccer, since catching was allowed to any member of the team. There was, however, a restriction on running with the ball. This could only be done back from the mark at which the catch was taken; if the catcher wanted to go

forward he could do so only as a follow-up to his kick ahead. The revolutionary thing that young Ellis did was to run forward with the ball in his hands." – WRHR001

Reyburn then forgot about Ellis and went on to write the history of the game.

1979 – THE WORLD OF RUGBY

In the 1979 book on the history of the game, leading journalist John Reason, together with Carwyn James, one of the finest coaches Britain has ever seen, and both renowned thinkers about the game, opened their dialogue with:

"The story about William Webb Ellis has never sounded very convincing. It is hard to believe that hundreds of boys at Rugby School suddenly cried Eureka, and stopped what they had being doing for years, and did something else, simply because one unexceptional and somewhat reluctant young footballer broke the rules of the game as it was played at the school in 1823." – JRWR007

They then linked up Rugby Football with folk football:

"There was nothing new about football, of course. That had been played for at least 2,000 years. There was nothing new about picking up the ball and running with it, either. That had been the essence of the game throughout its history. Indeed, if you study the history of football you will see that the one truly remarkable thing about Rugby football is not that it is a new game but that it is precisely the opposite, because it is the football which most closely resembles that played from before the time of the Romans and right through the Middle Ages." – JRWR011

The significance of this publication was the accompanying BBC television series that broadcast the folk football origin theory to the hundreds of thousands of viewers. The Webb Ellis origin theory was in rapid decline.

1991 – RUNNING WITH THE BALL – THE BIRTH OF RUGBY FOOTBALL

In a book about the early development of Rugby Union, Jenny Macrory, the archivist of Rugby School, ascribes the origin of Rugby Union to the Webb Ellis event and discusses the early development of the game. Her sources and text are selective in support of this, but she is unable to avoid casting doubt onto the Webb Ellis event in her summary:

"The big mistake made by the Old Rugbeian Society was in the wording of the plaque which they decided to erect on the Close in 1900 to pronounce their understandable

pride in the game which had developed there. They intended to celebrate the game, but instead created a myth." – JMRB035

"It was a brilliant piece of public relations, and captured the collective imagination as surely as the most carefully orchestrated modern advertising campaign.
The popular history of Rugby Football was written in 1900 quite literally in a tablet of stone. The report of the committee carefully noting the gradual acceptance of the carrying game was forgotten, and the big bang story was born." – JMRB036

1999 – THE UNION GAME – A RUGBY HISTORY

Author Sean Smith is a bit more brutal with his dismissal of the Webb Ellis event in his book 'The Union Game – A Rugby History' published in 1999 to accompany another BBC series. The series was produced in Wales by Dafydd Llyr James with the script written by Professor David Smith.

"...The Webb Ellis Trophy... named after the pupil at Rugby School who, in the best traditions of comic strip heroism, caught the ball and ran with it in 1823. At least that is what the public-school influences controlling Rugby Union wanted everyone to believe when they literally etched the name of Webb Ellis in stone in 1900. The Webb Ellis myth was assured when they set a commemorative plaque in the Headmaster's Wall in the Close at Rugby School." – SSUG014

The book then goes on to name the origins as most likely to be the Roman Folk Football game of harpastum:

"In truth credit should probably go to some anonymous Roman centurion, creator of the ancient game of harpastum. Then again, the Romans almost certainly stole the idea from the Greeks, as harpastum is derived from a Greek word meaning 'to snatch'. Harpastum was a sort of organised mêlée in which two sets of players endeavoured to catch a ball and to be the first to carry it over goal-lines marked at either end of the playing surface." – SSUG014

1999 – WILLIAM WEBB ELLIS – FICTION OR FACTS

Another study undertaken at the dawn of the new millennium by South African Professor Floris van der Merwe boldly devotes an entire book to the origin.

"This step by the investigating committee appears to be the origin of the popular misconception that Ellis "created" the game in 1823. To the critical observer, however, this story is not convincing and is today regarded as pure myth. Why would a group of children all of a sudden discover a "new game" and in the process change their

tradition simply because one person broke the existing rules? Furthermore, there is no primary evidence to support this story." – FMWW001

In his conclusion on the founding of the game, the wheel has turned full circle and the origin of the sport is once again accredited to folk football.

"For the critic, there is no rationale behind Bloxam's story. If he could make the mistake about Ellis, he could possibly have unearthed from memory an inaccurate picture of Rugby's pattern of play. The sources consulted, agree that schools football descended from folk football." – FMWW013

2006 – A GAME FOR HOOLIGANS – THE HISTORY OF RUGBY UNION

In 'A Game for Hooligans – The History of Rugby Union', published by Mainstream in 2006, Huw Richards briefly takes the time to name folk football as the origin of the sport before consigning William Webb Ellis to the bin later in the chapter…

"Seven varieties of football emerged from the common origin of pre-modern folk games." – HRGH016

"Whether or not rugby union is inimical to the arts, it has been careless with its history. It has enshrined its dubious myth of foundation in naming its World Cup trophy after William Webb Ellis." – HRGH021

2015 – THE OVAL WORLD – A GLOBAL HISTORY OF RUGBY

The most recent publication on the history of the sport was written by Tony Collins, Professor of History and a former Director of the International Centre for Sports History and Culture at De Montfort University.

"The Oval World is the first full-length history of rugby on a world scale – from it's origins in the village-based football games of medieval times to the globalised sport of the twenty-first century…" – TCOW0-dj-sum

2015 – WORLD RUGBY WEBSITE

The last bastion of the Webb Ellis theory lies with the game's governing body, World Rugby.

"The legend of William Webb Ellis, who is credited with first picking up the football and running with it, has doggedly survived the countless revisionist theories since that day at

Rugby School in 1823. That the Game should have its origins in an act of spirited defiance is somehow appropriate." – laws.worldrugby.org – 20 November 2015 – WRSS20151120-lw

2015 – RUGBY FOOTBALL UNION WEBSITE

However, this theory does not filter down to some of its member unions, which include the Rugby Football Union Museum at Twickenham. In its educational programme, the museum gives the origins of Rugby Union as folk football in 9th Century England.

"Association football, Rugby Union and Rugby League all have their roots in mob football that has been played on the streets and fields of Britain since, at least, the 9th Century." – RFUS20160422

SUMMARY – The earliest book on the history of football by Routledge set the scene for future historians. Routledge was a supporter of the 'Rugby School Rules' which was the code under which Rugby Union was being played at the time and, although he was undecided about the origin of this game, he listed various forms of folk football in his dialogue. Other historians followed in his footsteps, including Shearman who attributed the origin of Rugby Union to folk football, and Marshall, who attributed it to the Roman game of harpastum. The Old Rugbeian Society, unhappy with the folk football theory, published a report on the 'Origin of Rugby Football' naming William Webb Ellis as its founder. This was accepted universally at the time, but with years gone by the theory has been questioned. Today historians have discarded Webb Ellis as the founder and dubbed the event as a myth. The last two major remaining strongholds claiming William Webb Ellis as the founder of Rugby Union are Rugby School and World Rugby.

CONCLUSION – In its entire existence there have been two main beliefs for the origin of rugby football:

1 Folk Football (Earliest Possible Origin)

2 William Webb Ellis event (Earliest Accepted Origin)

FOOTNOTE – There we have it, two theories – the sport's governing body, and may I add Rugby School too, clinging to the Webb Ellis theory and everyone else saying that folk football must be the origin. I'm looking at my Webb Ellis signature and thinking that I need to sort this out so that I can begin the story of the sport of Rugby Union in my Museum. So that we can decide on which theory is true, what we need to do next is analyse both theories. But let's take some time before we move on and as we are turning the page, let's sing to the tune of 'We're off to see the wizard, the wonderful wizard of Oz……….."

"We're off to check out William"
and Folk Football as a game
Which one is the origin?
Webb Ellis or Harpastum?

La la la la la la la la la la la la la la la la la la la la la la la la la la la....

CHAPTER 3 – IS FOLK FOOTBALL THE ORIGIN OF RUGBY UNION?

AIM – To look at the belief held by modern day historians that the origin of rugby lies with folk football. What do the sources of reference for the early history of football tell us and how do they relate to the game played at Rugby School at its earliest accepted origin?

Where shall we start? If we refer back to the recording of the game, the early histories of football all mentioned folk football, so let's start with those.

Although Routledge's 1867 Handbook of Football covered the many versions of folk football, he stated plainly that he knew not of the origin. Therefore, the first publication we will look at is Montague Shearman and James E Vincent's 'Foot-ball – Its History for Five Centuries', published in 1885 by Field & Tuer. In their preface, Shearman & Vincent state:

"There also resulted a theory, which was not adopted without anxious argument, that the games of football now in vogue owe their origin almost entirely to the public schools; and that in the public schools rules were the consequence of circumstances and environment. At the same time football has a history which has been faithfully followed." – MSFC0pf.v

The important words to note in the above statement are 'almost entirely', meaning that not every form of football played in the public schools was developed internally within the various schools. There was an exception and later on in the book the authors identify Football at Rugby School as being the original folk football game (MSFC048).

In the opening chapter, the authors briefly discuss the possibility that the history of football had two legends. Of one – (folk) football as played in ancient times – referring to the Isle of Purbeck quarrymen game, they say:

"But the origin of the practice, both in that locality and in some other parts of the country where it is known to have been followed, is shrouded in antiquity; and there is little evidence to show that this practice caused the rise of football, instead of having arisen at a time when the game itself was well known." – MSFC004

The other legend was of Barbarian hordes kicking around severed heads, including in the Chester game *"...the head of a Dane is still stated to have been the original ball used in the game."* (MSFC005). Shearman & Vincent however dismiss that this was the origin:

"...we can still comfort ourselves by feeling certain that football had no such horrible origin..." – MSFC005

They do, however, draw similarities between folk football and Rugby Union:

"Sometimes we hear of goals a mile or so apart; often the arena of play was a street or a high road, sometimes a whole town; and the attacking party with the ball would try and sneak round by bye-streets in order to escape notice, and plant the ball unawares through the window or against the post which was fixed as the goal. The game, in short, when played in a confined space, was none other than a rough form of the present Rugby Union football, without the rules and prohibitions which have now reduced to order and civilised that game." – MSFC012

The book continues to discuss various forms of folk football during and after the 'Puritan' era, before dealing exclusively with the 'History of Football in the Public Schools'. The opening passage of that chapter is worth recording here because it identifies Rugby School as being the sole surviving location for the original game. However, in its entirety, the book fails to pinpoint what the original game actually was.

"It is vastly to the credit of cricket and of football that they should have survived the Puritan deluge and the decay of the athletic spirit at the end of the last century, and not have been laid in limbo together with stoolball, cambuc, and other games wherein the hearts of out forefathers rejoiced. The survival indicates an exceeding fitness. Still the storm of Puritanical hatred had been enough to kill even hardier plants than these, unless there had been some quiet haunts in which they existed unnoticed and unmolested. As to the pastimes of the 'prentice boys they perished; but in the quiet privacy of the country and in the almost monastic seclusion of some of our ancient public schools they continued to exist.
For some reason or other, the foundation of Laurence Sheriff, at Rugby, was the locality in which, what we now call the Rugby game, but which, for reasons above mentioned, appears in reality to have been the pristine form of the game, was preserved. Now, since of every effect there is a cause, and since of this particular effect history supplies us no cause that we are aware of, it becomes necessary to have recourse to conjecture; and since conjecture, to be probable, must proceed upon some sound basis, it seems to follow, that in order to discover why the game, distinguished by an absence of rules, survived in Rugby School, an inquiry should be made whether the conditions of football at Rugby were not different from what they were elsewhere. The answer to this question, once formulated, is manifest. The conditions of football were different at Rugby from those which prevailed at other schools; or rather, to put the matter in language paradoxical in appearance but literally correct, the conditions of the game were normal at Rugby and abnormal everywhere else. In fact, the original form of football, – for it is the simplest, – is of such a nature that it can hardly be played except in a wide open

space. Such a space existed at Rugby from the beginning, but not at the other great public schools." – MSFC047

After a short summary of the Eton, Winchester & Charterhouse games, they close the paragraph with:

"Therefore it was natural in each particular school the rules of the game should be settled by the capacities of the playground; and as these were infinitely various in character, so were the games various." – MSFC049

Simplifying the conclusions drawn by Shearman & Vincent: there were many forms of ancient football that all derived from one source – the original game – but they don't actually know what the original game was. The sole survivor of this form of football was played at Rugby School, owing to the school's remoteness in the country. Several other public schools played various different forms of football that each differed from the original game and evolved as a result of the nature of the environment in which the game was played.

In 1887, Shearman published 'Athletics & Football', in which he once again ascribed the origin of Rugby Union Football to the original game:

"Probably the name 'football' was first used to describe the ball itself, and meant a ball which was big enough to be kicked and could be kicked with the foot. The game of football was the game played with this kind of ball, and it was simple to an extreme degree. The goals were two bushes, posts, houses or any objects fixed upon at any distance apart from a few score yards to a few miles. The ball was placed mid-way between the two goals at starting, the players (of any number) divided into two sides, and it was the business of either side to get the ball by force or strategy up to or through the goal of the opposite side. When confined to a street, or field of play, it is obvious that the sport was the original form of what is now known as the Rugby Union game." – MSAF250

What he says is that ancient football had three rules:

1. The ball starts on the half way line
2. There are two sides
3. The ball needs to go through the goal, by any method, for a score to be registered

In the same chapter he mentions several different forms of folk football:

Greek football & two types of Roman football – MSAF246

Chester football – where they originally used the head of a Dane – MSAF247

Derby football – which celebrated a victory over the Romans in the third century – MSAF247

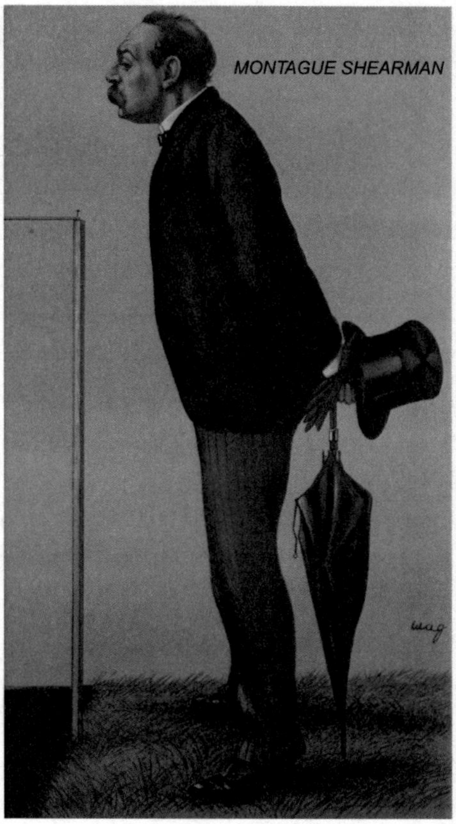

Isle of Purbeck football – where the free quarrymen kicked a football over the ground they had claimed – MSAF247

Fitzstephen's Shrove Tuesday 'boys in the field' football – MSAF248

London boys and 'prentices football' – MSAF248

London large ball football, played at the time of Edward II – MSAF248

Elizabethan football – MSAF251

Cornish hurling – described by Carew as simply being football with much running and little or no kicking – MSAF257

Camp ball – MSAF260

Football at Scone in Perthshire: *"The game was the same as that known as 'hurling' in Cornwall, as 'camp-ball' in the eastern counties, and football elsewhere"…"The game was an annual one between the bachelors and the married men, and the object of the married men was to hang it, that is to put it three times into a small hole in the moor which was the 'dool'."* – MSAF261

I mention all of the above types of folk football because it is worth taking note of the diversity. What Shearman is saying here is that because all of these sports used a ball, that they were the same, which is like saying that chess and monopoly are the same game because they are played on a board, that darts and archery are the same because they are aiming pointy things at a target, and that boxing and wrestling are the same because they are based on two people fighting in a ring. He also goes on to say that:

"The origin of the Scone game, like the origin of the annual game at Chester, Derby, Kingston, Corfe Castle, and elsewhere, is shrouded in obscurity…" – MSAF261

In other words he hasn't got a clue how any of the games originated, but had previously (and also a page later) made up his mind that their origins were the same:

"… it is obvious that the sport was the original form of what is now known as the Rugby Union game." – MSAF251

"However to return to our history. There is no doubt that hurling, football, and camp-ball were in their origin the same." – MSAF262

He says this in spite of the fact that the games were in some cases played hundreds of miles apart, with different equipment, on different sized areas, with different rules. He doesn't know how they started, but says that they all originated from the same game, whose origin is shrouded in obscurity. All of these games then became the same game – Rugby Union – even though one of those games was played with sticks.

The confusion in this publication and Routledge's earlier 'Handbook of Football' lies in the fact that the authors were unable to differentiate between the various forms of folk football. Even though they are clearly different games, they cannot fathom that they might have evolved separately from unconnected sources. It must be remembered that Shearman's book appeared just five years after the death of Charles Darwin, whose 'On the Origin of the Species' book ran to 6 editions, the last having been published in 1872. It's very possible that Shearman drew inspiration from Darwin's work and attempted to draw his own 'tree of life' adapted to the origin of football.

In 1892 the Reverend Frank Marshall wrote the first complete history dedicated to rugby football. Over 500 pages long, it is still the major reference work for rugby football historians. Unfortunately, in the first chapter of the book, Marshall states that he uses Shearman's book as a work of reference.

Let's start at the beginning:

CHAPTER 1

The Origin of the Game

"It is not within the purpose of the present work to give a detailed and exhaustive record of the ancient games of football or to compile a history of the game as played in this country for so many centuries. The ancient records have been so exhaustively searched into by Mr. Montague Shearman, and embodied by him in the Badminton Series, in addition to a work by the same author in conjunction with Mr. James E. Vincent "Football: Its History for Two Centuries..." – FMRU001

Marshall's book was published in two further editions, in 1894 and 1925 (updated by Tosswill). The opening chapter remains the same in both editions, as does the error he makes where he refers to Shearman and Vincent's book as *"Football: Its History for Two Centuries"*, when it should read *"Football: Its History for Five Centuries"*. Did Marshall even read the book in the first place?

Towards the end of the chapter he concludes:

"Uniting the extracts, references, and descriptions as above, we can summarise the history of football as played in this island as follows, viz :- That the Romans, who occupied this island during the first four centuries of the Christian era, played at a game of ball called harpastum, which game presented the special features of carrying the ball and the scrummage, found in no other modern game of football save in the Rugby game; that it can be traced back to Roman times that a game of football was played in Britain; and that, as far as can be gathered from tradition, all games then played were characterised by much carrying and little kicking of the ball. It can also be concluded that a game of ball – passing under various names of "football," "hurling," "camp-ball," and the like – has always been a popular sport of the lower orders of society; and though such games have differed somewhat from each other, they have all concurred in being "carrying" games. Indeed, little or no trace of kicking the ball can be found, and in some cases there has been an actual prohibition of kicking altogether. Further, other distinctive features of the Rugby game can be traced, as, for instance, the forbidding of the passing forward of the ball, which clearly demonstrates that the game as at present played under Rugby Union code is the legitimate refinement of the rough and crude games of our ancestors. Nowhere can there be found any trace whatever of a game assimilating, however remotely, to the kicking game of the Association Code. In making this assertion we have no intention of indulging in disparagement of the Association game. If the name of football can in the strict meaning of the word be applied to any game the Association game can legitimately claim an almost exclusive right to be

termed football; but if it be a reproach as is often so alleged, against the Rugby game, that it contains much handling but little kicking of the ball, it is on the other hand, the glory and the privilege of Rugby Unionists to know that the game which they so dearly love, and which they have spent so much time in developing and perfecting, is in its main features the same game that has been played in this island for centuries. The Rugby game is, in fact, the most ancient of all popular sports of the present day." – FMRU012

So he's saying that rugby began with harpastum, then developed into hurling, camp-ball and the like, and then became Rugby.

Earlier in the same chapter, he says:

"The Romans may or may not, have introduced the harpastum into Britain. There is no historical evidence to show that they actually did so…" – FMRU003

Which potentially contradicts what he says later on (from the above extract):

"That the Romans, who occupied this island during the first four centuries of the Christian era, played at a game of ball called harpastum…" – FMRU012

Even if the Romans brought harpastum to Britain, or found it played by the native Britons when they arrived, unless it lay in hibernation under the Close at Rugby School for 1400 years, then there is no link to the game of Football at Rugby School. It is important to note that in all of the forms of folk football mentioned in both Shearman's & Marshall's books, not one of them is described to have a crossbar. The aim of Football at Rugby School at the time of Webb Ellis was to kick the ball between the uprights and over the crossbar, as Matthew Bloxam says about his time at the school (1813–1820):

"…for it was by means of these placed kicks that most of the goals were in those days kicked…" – ORSR010

Goals scored by kicking the ball over the crossbar and between the posts were the only method of scoring ever recorded for Football at Rugby School. In later chapters it will become apparent as to why this is so important.

As previously mentioned, in his 1899 book 'Football', Shearman concedes that he was incorrect in his assumption that folk football had survived at Rugby School.

Modern day historians, such as Floris van der Merwe and Christopher Rowley, who will be referred to later on, say that because folk football was played with a similar ball to that used in rugby, that it was a natural forerunner of Football at Rugby School. However, as was the case for Shearman & Marshall, no links have been established.

SUMMARY - There is no evidence of a link from the ancient forms of folk football to that played at Rugby School prior to and at the time of William Webb Ellis. Both Shearman and Marshall have contradicted themselves on the origin of the game. In a nutshell, they say that all forms of folk football started with one original game. Marshall states that this original game is the game that the Romans called harpastum. They say that this original game then branched out into many forms with many different rules, before returning back to one game – Football at Rugby School. They do not know how the games were founded but can be sure that they were the forebears of Rugby Football because of the similarities with respect to the carrying of the ball. Both authors fail to prove that a link exists between these forms of football and the game played at Rugby School. They have proven that ancient football existed, however, not one of these forms of football involved kicking a ball between the uprights and over a crossbar, which in the early 1800s was the aim of the game at Rugby School. We must believe both authors to be incorrect, and we assume that they were swayed by the then recent achievements of Charles Darwin and his theory of evolution.

CONCLUSION – It is highly improbable for there to be a link between folk football and Football at Rugby School.

FOOTNOTE – if the origin of Rugby Union does not lie with folk football, then surely it must lay with William Webb Ellis. To the tune of Rod Stewart's classic 'Sailing', 3 – 2 – 1...........

It must be Ellissssssssss..........
William Webb Ellisssssss.........
Who invented...... the Rugby game
It must be Ellisssssss
William Ellissssss
And we love him, he's to blame

CHAPTER 4 – ANALYSIS OF THE WILLIAM WEBB ELLIS EVENT

AIM – To analyse the William Webb Ellis event. Did it really happen and if it did, is it the origin of Rugby Union?

BACKGROUND

The theory that the William Webb Ellis event was the origin of Rugby Union didn't begin in 1823, but instead began 74 years later in 1897 with the publication of a report by a sub-committee of the Old Rugbeian Society called 'The Origin of Rugby Football'. The conclusion of that report is that the origin of Rugby Union began with William Webb Ellis in 1823.

".....that this was in all probability done in the latter half of 1823 by Mr. W Webb Ellis, who is credited by Mr. Bloxam with the invention and whose 'unfair practices' were (according to Mr. Harris) the subject of general remark at the time." – ORSR022

The only known portrait of William Webb Ellis, 1857

THE 1897 REPORT ON THE ORIGIN OF RUGBY

More of Webb Ellis later, but firstly, because the report is so important in pinpointing the Webb Ellis event as the origin of Rugby Union, let's look at the report in its entirety. Why was it commissioned? Who wrote the report? What are its conclusions? Are these conclusions correct? Did it take into account all of the available information? There are so many questions to be asked that we'd better make a start on it pronto, and where better to start than at its beginning:

"In the "Athletics and Football" volume of the Badminton Library – in almost every respect a most painstaking and praiseworthy book – the author, Mr. Montague Shearman commits himself to certain statements about the Rugby game which we venture to consider misleading, if not altogether erroneous." – ORSR003

WHY WAS THE REPORT COMMISSIONED?

Montague Shearman knew how to kick up a storm. The below paragraph in the Football section of his book in the chapter 'History' upset the Old Rugbeians, who had studied and played the game at the school that had given its name to the sport now called Rugby Union. Rugbeians had always believed that this was their game, a game they had invented and showed the world how to play. This was their sport, but this was Shearman's conclusion:

"Now at the present day every large school has a good large grass playground either in the grounds of the school itself or within convenient reach; but in the olden times little or no provision for 'playing fields' appears to have been made by pious or other founders. One school alone seems to have owned almost from its foundation a wide open grass playground of ample dimensions, and that school was Rugby; hence it happens as we should have expected, that at Rugby School alone do we find that the original game survived almost in it's primitive shape." – MSAF271

From the opening paragraph we can surmise that the reason that the report was commissioned was to dispute Montague Shearman's claim that the 'original' version of folk football survived at Rugby School because it had a large playground (wide open spaces) and because Rugby Union at the time of his book had similarities with folk football, in that you were allowed to carry the ball. The Old Rugbeian Society found Montague Shearman's conclusions to be *"misleading, if not altogether erroneous"*.

WHAT WAS THE PURPOSE OF THE REPORT?

The purpose of the report was to place the 'Origin of Rugby Football' at Rugby School. Its aim according to the opening paragraph was:

"... to investigate these statements, and also to enquire into the account of the origin of our game put forward on more than one occasion by the late Mr. Matthew Holbeche Bloxam..." – ORSR003

The report needed to discredit Shearman so that the origin of Rugby Union could be placed at Rugby School. To do this the sub-committee needed to prove two things:

1 – That Rugby School did not originally have wide open spaces where a game of folk football could have survived.

2 – That Football at Rugby School was mainly a kicking game, which then developed into a handling game.

DID THE REPORT PROVE THAT THERE WERE NO OPEN SPACES FOR FOLK FOOTBALL TO SURVIVE?

Yes it did. On the subject of the open spaces, the committee suggested that Shearman should have consulted an Old Rugbeian on this matter. They name the three authors of the Winchester, Eton & Harrow chapters from Shearman's book and state:

"He does not, however, appear to have consulted any Old Rugbeian to the same extent with reference to the Rugby game, and it is probably due to this fact that, as we hold, he has fallen into error. In his other book on the same subject, 'Football : Its History for Five Centuries', (Field & Tuer 1885), written, as he informs us, in conjunction with Mr. Vincent, he discussed the origin of the various forms of School football: and the conclusion arrived at in that work was that 'in each particular school the rules of the game were settled by the capacity of the play-ground; and that as these were infinitely various in character, so were the games various.' " – ORSR003

The report is selectively quoting Shearman here, although at least getting the title of his 1885 work correct. In 'Foot-ball – Its History for Five Centuries', Shearman did state that Rugby School was the exception to this rule, and in 1887 he is just confirming his earlier diagnosis. The big picture, however, is that in that book Shearman makes Rugby School the public scapegoat, so that his folk football origin theory can be traced back to ancient times and the 'original game', because as shown in the previous chapter, it's almost impossible to link folk football to being the origin of Rugby Union.

The report argues its case about the school having *"from its foundation a wide open grass playground of ample dimensions"* (MSAF271) by listing the various additions to Rugby Close (the area in which Football was played) and publishing maps that highlight these. The school had moved from the middle of town with no playground to a Manor House with fields on the edge of town in 1750 (MBRN003).

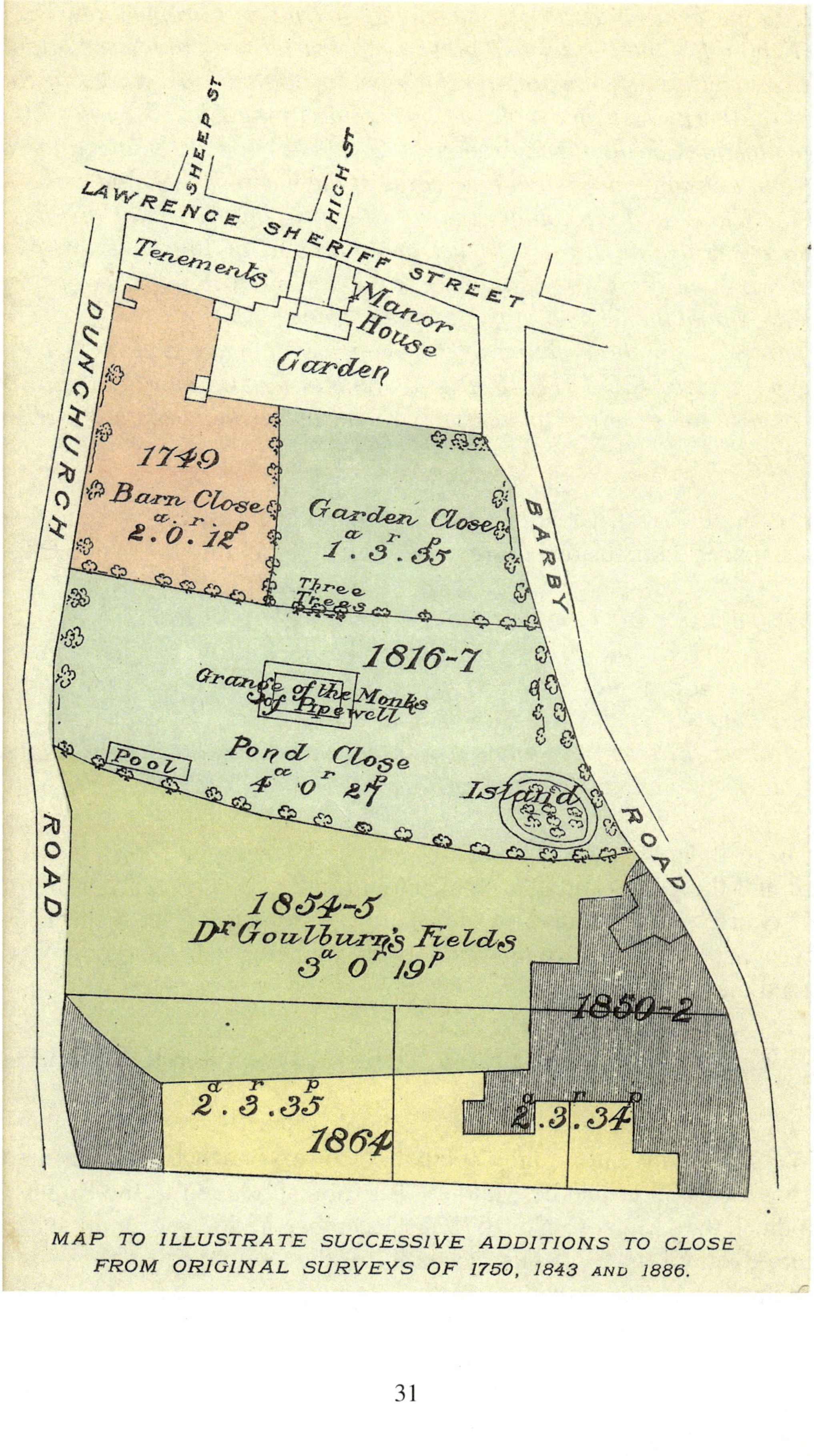

MAP TO ILLUSTRATE SUCCESSIVE ADDITIONS TO CLOSE FROM ORIGINAL SURVEYS OF 1750, 1843 AND 1886.

The report also draws on the article written in the Meteor by the local historian Matthew Holbeche Bloxam who stated that there was a limited amount of space for play:

"An article in the Times newspaper, the leading journal of Europe, a few weeks past, on the Rugby School Football Rules and play, as contrasted with the Association Rules, has prompted me to write a few words on the game of football, as played at Rugby in my time, 1813–1820. The last time I played at Bigside in the Close was just 60 years ago, and my recollections of the game extend to 67 years... In 1813, the available space for the play-ground was not more than four acres at the most...The island was in a separate field from the Close, and the southern part of the present Close was divided into fields, and formed a small dairy farm. Cricket and Football at Bigside were played at the north-west corner of the Close, adjoining the Dunchurch Road. One of the goals was erected on the site of the Chapel, not then in existence.
When preparations for the erection of the chapel were made and the ground enclosed for that purpose, circa A.D.1817–18, Bigside both at Cricket and Football was removed to that part of the close lying immediately South of the headmaster's garden wall." – ORSR008

The report continues with Bloxam's account of Football at Rugby School then breaks for its 'open spaces' conclusion before moving seamlessly into the Webb Ellis theory.

"In the passage just quoted another blow is given to Mr. Shearman's cherished theory, that Rugby preserved "the primitive game". We have already shewn that until 1749 Rugby was without any play-ground for football at all: and when the purchase of the manor-house and its enclosures supplied the deficiency, the game that was played (according to Mr. Bloxam's testimony) was not the game that Rugby knows now, but something more resembling Association Football" – ORSR009

There we have it, in a nutshell and in one small paragraph, until 1749 there was no playground and the game was like Association football (soccer), according to Matthew Bloxam of course. But just in case we've missed something let's check out how the report proves that Football at Rugby School was a kicking game and how William Webb Ellis invented the running game.

DID THE REPORT PROVE THAT RUGBY WAS A KICKING GAME?

This account of early Football at Rugby School is what gave birth to the legend that William Webb Ellis invented rugby football. Correspondence with former pupils and extracts from the 1880 article by Matthew Bloxam, submitted to the Rugby School old boys periodical the 'Meteor' No 157 22 December 1880, appear in the report. The editor's introduction to Bloxam's account of the Webb Ellis event is of critical importance because he states that this is the *"origin of the present rugby game"*:

"We now come to Mr. Bloxam's account of the origin of the present rugby game, which is of such importance that we print it in extenso."

"In the latter half of 1823, some 57 years ago, originated, though without premeditation, that change in one of the rules which more than any other has since distinguished the Rugby school game from the Association Rules.

A boy of the name of Ellis - William Webb Ellis - a town boy and a foundationer, who at the age of nine entered the school after the midsummer holidays in 1816, who in the second half-year of 1823 was, I believe, a præposter, whilst playing Bigside at football in that half-year, caught the ball in his arms. This being so, according to the then rule, he ought to have retired back as far as he pleased, without parting with the ball, for the combatants on the opposite side could only advance to the spot where he had caught the ball, and were unable to rush forward until he had either punted it or placed it for someone else to kick, for it was by means of these placed kicks that most of the goals were in those days kicked, but the moment the ball touched the ground, the opposite side might rush on. Ellis, for the first time, disregarded this rule, and on catching the ball, instead of retiring backwards, rushed forwards with the ball in his hands towards the opposite goal, with what result as to the game I know not, neither do I know how this infringement of a well-known rule was followed up, or when it became, as it is now, the standing rule. Mr. Ellis was high up in the school, and as to scholarship of fair average abilities. He left the school in the summer of 1825, being the second Rugby Exhibitioner of that year, and was entered at Brasenose College, Oxford. He subsequently took Holy Orders, and at a later period became Incumbent of the church of St. Clement Danes, Strand. He died on the Continent some years ago. When at school, though in a high form, Mr. Ellis was not what we should call a 'swell,' at least none of his compeers considered him as such; he had, however, plenty of assurance, and was ambitious of being thought something of. In fact he did an act which if a fag had ventured to have done, he would probably have received more kicks than commendations. How oft it is that such small matters lead to great results!" – ORSR009

The report continues and it's worth quoting the text that follows for the conclusions reached by the editor:

"Mr. Bloxam's very circumstantial account of Mr Ellis's exploit, though not that of an eye-witness (for he had left the school some three years before) cannot be ignored, and though we have been unable to procure any first hand evidence of the occurrence, we are inclined to give it our support. Some one must have broken through the rule against running with the ball, and Mr. Bloxam (who is a fellow-townsman of Mr. Ellis and was at the time, we believe, pursuing his legal studies in Rugby) had evidently satisfied himself of the accuracy of the story. He had previously broached the subject, as he tells us in a letter headed "Football and Athletics" to the Meteor (No. 104) of October 10, 1876 by writing to the Standard (in which a discussion on the game had been taking

place) to controvert the belief, expressed by one of its correspondents that the Rugby game, at present played at Rugby, was 'of great and unknown antiquity'. He then stated, that instead of this being the case, the present game, so far as the rules authorised the ball being carried by hand, the holder running with it, was unknown during the time he was at school, viz. 1813 to 1820, and went to say that he thought it was introduced in Dr. Arnold's time. In the letter to the Meteor, however, he says he had "since ascertained" that the change originated, in the manner already detailed above, in the second half year of 1823, that at first it did not succeed, but was soon set aside, and was not again introduced until Dr Arnold's mastership 1828–1842." – ORSR010

The next section in the report is dedicated to the correspondence of former pupils and it contains most interesting information in relation to the game, how it was played and the rules. One letter is from a former pupil, Thomas Harris, who was familiar with Webb Ellis and whose time at Rugby School overlapped Ellis'. The letter was written to Henry Homer who had contacted Harris on behalf of the ORS.

"1. Picking up and running with the ball in hand was distinctly forbidden. If a player caught the ball on a rebound from the ground or from the stroke of a hand, he was allowed to take a few steps so as to give effect to a 'Drop-kick,' but no more: subject of course to interruption from the adverse players. I remember Mr. William Webb Ellis perfectly. He was an admirable cricketer, but was generally regarded as inclined to take unfair advantages at Football. I should not quote him in any way as an authority.

2. If the ball was caught in the hands from a kick, the catcher was entitled to 'place try' at goal, retiring a sufficient distance from the place where the catch was made.

3. All laying hands upon and holding a player was strictly forbidden under any circumstances.

I do not remember any other material points in connection with Football: a grand game as I used to consider it, as formerly played. I may add that my brother John Harris, who left rugby in 1832, and who was a devoted lover of the game, agrees with me in the particulars given above. He happens to be at this time staying with me." – ORSR020

The ORS wrote again looking for more information and the reply from Thomas Harris was as follows:

"I'm afraid that I can add but little to the recollections of Rugby Football which I gave in my letter to Homer. As to Mr. W. Webb Ellis and his practices, you must observe that I was several years his junior, and had not either reasons or opportunities for closely observing his manner of play. I am sure, however, that it was very generally regarded as unfair by the leading players of the day. It may be that his practice of running with the ball, which Mr. Matthew Bloxam speaks of as having been invented by him, was the

point objected to; but of this I cannot speak from my own observation. I may add that in the matches played by boys in the lower part of the School, while I was myself a junior, the cry of "Hack him over" was always raised against any player who was seen to be running with the ball in his hands. Our laws in those days were unwritten and traditionary, so that I can give no authority beyond custom." – ORSR022

Harris confirms that Webb Ellis is a cheat, which backs up Matthew Bloxam's account of Webb Ellis running forward with the ball, and the committee consider that they have proven that Football at Rugby School was a kicking game before it became a handling game. The report's editor then comments on the Webb Ellis event after receiving Thomas Harris' second letter:

"It may, we think, be fairly considered to be proved from the foregoing statements, that (1) in 1820 the form of football in vogue at Rugby was something approximating more closely to Association than to what is known as Rugby football to-day, (2) that at some date between 1820 and 1830 the innovation was introduced of running with the ball, (3) that this was in all probability done in the latter half of 1823 by Mr. W. Webb Ellis, who is credited by Mr Bloxam with the invention and whose 'unfair practices' were (according to Mr. Harris) the subject of general remark at the time. To this we would add that the innovation was regarded as of doubtful legality for some time, and only gradually became accepted as part of the game, but obtained a customary status between 1830 and 1840, and was duly legalized first by Bigside Levee in 1841–42 (as stated by Judge Hughes) and finally by the Rules of 1846 (Appendix A)." – ORSR022

WHO WAS BLOXAM'S SOURCE?

Matthew Bloxam's younger brother John Rouse Bloxam was still alive in 1876 and it is generally thought that as John was a contemporary of Webb Ellis, leaving Rugby School at around 1826 (to be confirmed), it is probable that Bloxam senior obtained the Webb Ellis information from him.

WHAT WERE THE CONSEQUENCES OF THE REPORT?

Firstly, Montague Shearman puts his hands up and says he was wrong. In the first edition of his book titled 'Football', published in 1899, he states in his chapter on the history of the game, a previous version of which appeared in 'Athletics and Football':

"Since this chapter was written, in 1887, a sub-committee of the Old Rugbeian Society (consisting of Messrs. H. F. Wilson, H.H. Child, A.G. Guillemard, and H.L. Stephen) has paid me the compliment of making a searching investigation, both from historical documents and from inquiry from living Old Rugbeians, with the view to testing my theory that 'at Rugby alone was the old running and collaring game kept up.' The result of their inquiries has been embodied in a pamphlet entitled 'The Origin of Rugby

Football,' and published by Mr. Laurence, of Rugby. The writers point out that I was incorrect in my statement that 'Rugby seems to have owned almost from its foundation a wide open grass playground of ample dimensions,' and show that the school had no regular playground until 1749, when it obtained one of 2 a o r. 12 p., and no really 'ample playground' until 1816–17; and the net result of their researches is summed up as follows..." – MSFT034

Then he quotes directly from the Old Rugbeian Society report:

"It may, we think, be fairly considered to be proved from the foregoing statements that (1) in 1820 the form of football in vogue at Rugby was something approximating more closely to Association than what is known as Rugby football to-day; (2) that at some date between 1820 and 1830 the innovation was introduced of running with the ball; (3) that this was in all probability done in the latter half of 1823 by Mr. Webb Ellis...To this we would add that the innovation was regarded as of doubtful legality for some time, and only gradually became accepted as part of the game, but obtained a customary status between 1830 and 1840, and was duly legalised first by Bigside Levee in 1841–42 (as stated by Judge Hughes), and finally by the rules of 1846." – MSFT035

A year later, the Old Rugbeian Society, confident of no opposition, lay the plaque in the wall of the Headmaster's Garden at Rugby School.

It is this plaque more than anything that has perpetuated the William Webb Ellis event as being the origin of Rugby Union. So where do we go from here? Do we accept the report as having proven the origin of Rugby Union? Or shall we check out its conclusions to see if they are correct? I find that the best way to analyse something is to ask questions, so let's start asking questions relating to this report to see if we can find the answers, and let's keep asking questions until we are happy that we've found them.

Let's start at the beginning and look at Shearman's claims. If Shearman's first edition of Athletics & Football was published in 1887 and his chapter on the history of Rugby Union remained the same, then we should be asking this question:

WHY DID IT TAKE EIGHT YEARS (UNTIL 1895) FOR THE REPORT TO BE COMMISSIONED?

I believe that the reason for this is that the report was actually commissioned to discredit the chapter 'Origin of the Game' in the first 'complete' rugby history by the Reverend

Frank Marshall, ‘Football – The Rugby Union game’, first published in 1892. In that book Marshall had leaned heavily on Shearman’s work for his references to the origin, but had come up with the conclusion that Rugby had evolved from the game the Romans had called harpastum.

“That the Romans, who occupied this island during the first four centuries of the Christian era, played at a game of ball called harpastum, which game presented the special features of carrying the ball and the scrummage, found in no other modern game of football save in the Rugby game…” – FMRU012

Whilst Shearman was non-committal in pointing the finger at what the ‘original game’ was, Marshall had pointed the finger at harpastum and moved the evolution goalposts firmly to the Italian invaders. To understand why the report targets Shearman instead of Marshall, we need to ask another question:

WHO COMPILED THE REPORT?

According to the front cover, it was a sub-committee of the Old Rugbeian Society. We have to turn to page 27 of the report to see who the members of this sub committee were. They were a group of four and before I tell you who they were, I’m going to give them a collective name. From now on, I’m going to call them ‘the plaque in the wall gang’.

Henry Francis Wilson, son of the Rev. William Greive Wilson, Rugby, attended Rugby School 1873–1878. He was a barrister by profession and was called to the bar in 1888 before embarking on a career in the civil service, chiefly as a legal advisor in the Colonial Office. He was appointed Secretary of the Trinidad Judicial Enquiry Commission in 1892 and was Secretary of the Orange River Colony in South Africa from 1902 to 1907. Other posts included that of Secretary of the Royal Colonial Institute (1915–21). He was knighted in 1908.

Herbert Henry Child was the second son of William Henry Child, Esq of Rugby. He attended Rugby School in 1870–1875 before moving on to Trinity College, Cambridge, where he obtained his B.A. in 1878. His profession was Barrister-at-Law, practising in Lincoln's Inn from 1882.

Arthur George Guillemard was a former pupil of Rugby School, 1859–1864. Guillemard had played for England in the first international in 1871, was a founder member of the RFU and had served on its committee as a Senior and Junior Vice-President, as Hon Treasurer, Hon Secretary and President. He was the fifth President of the Rugby Football Union (the previous four presidents had all been schooled at Rugby). At the inaugural meeting, it was his proposal to name the newly formed society the ‘Rugby

Football Union'. He refereed six internationals between 1877 and 1881 (JGPR103) and had acted as an umpire on the sidelines before referees were first appointed for matches in 1876. He was a solicitor.

Harry Lushington Stephen was the third son of Mr. Justice James Fitzjames Stephen. He attended Rugby School from 1874 to 1877 and studied at Trinity College, Cambridge. He was knighted in 1908 and his profession was barrister-at-law (Inner Temple 1885).

The plaque in the wall gang had of course all studied at Rugby School. Guillemard knew the game inside out, but more importantly, the Old Rugbeian had put pen to paper in Marshall's 1892 work in the second chapter 'A Bigside at Rugby', which included a large extract from Tom Brown's Schooldays. He also wrote Chapter VII 'The Foundation and Progress of the Rugby Football Union'. I believe that because the Rugby man was a contributing writer in that book, the sub committee of which he was a member couldn't be seen to be attacking Marshall's work. To have disputed Marshall's origin theories in the report would have discredited the whole of the book, including Guillemard's own chapters in which he sang the praises of Rugby School and the Rugby Football Union. So the Old Rugbeian Society had no other option but to contest the origin theories in Shearman's book instead, which is quoted as the main source of reference for Marshall's initial chapter on the origin of rugby.

Frank Marshall's first edition was published in 1892. It's possible that Arthur G Guillemard had a chat with Marshall and asked him to review his chapter on the origin. If he did, Marshall clearly didn't listen because two years later, just a year before the report was commissioned, the revised and enlarged edition of Marshall's book was published, with Chapter 1 remaining the same, errors included. Also rubbing salt into the Rugby School wounds in 1894 was Montague Shearman, publishing the fourth edition of 'Athletics and Football'.

To me it makes more sense that this is the reason why the Old Rugbeian Society commissioned the report, to halt the ever increasing momentum of the folk football origin theory, and in particular Marshall's theory that the game the Romans called harpastum was the origin of Rugby Football. We should now ask questions to see whether the information contained in the report is correct.

DID THE REPORT PROVE THAT THERE WERE NO OPEN SPACES FOR FOLK FOOTBALL TO SURVIVE?

Yes – the evidence is pretty conclusive. Until 1749 Rugby School was in the middle of the town and there was no dedicated playground for the boys. This information is readily available in sources relating to the history of Rugby School.

DID THE REPORT PROVE THAT RUGBY WAS A KICKING GAME?

Yes it did. Matthew Bloxam's 1880 article in the Meteor gives a good description of the nature of the game as played in his time at the school, 1813–1820. He states that those keeping goal were *"watching their opportunity for a casual kick"* (ORSR009), *"It was Football, and not Handball, plenty of hacking"* (ORSR009) and *"until he had either punted it or placed it for some one else to kick, for it was by means of these placed kicks that most of the goals were in those days kicked"* (ORSR010). Football at Rugby School was a kicking game, because it was illegal to pick a ball up off the floor, passing the ball was not allowed and running forward with the ball was taboo, so when the ball was on the floor there was no other choice than to kick it. If it was rolling forward towards you, maybe you could have stopped it with your hands then kicked or knocked it forward with your hands. But a kick would help the ball travel further and it was also a lot easier to do. Of course the most important factor – the objective of the game in Football at Rugby in 1813 was to score a goal by kicking the ball over the crossbar and between the posts. Football at Rugby School was a kicking game.

DID WEBB ELLIS REALLY RUN WITH THE BALL?

If what Webb Ellis did was so momentous, then it would have passed into Rugby School folklore and remained so. Yet, according to the report, pupils entering Rugby School less than five years after Ellis had left had never heard of him.

In writing in the Meteor in 1879, Matthew Bloxam says of the pupils around that time (1809):

"At this time boys not unfrequently continued at School ten or even twelve years, and traditions of a longer date were handed down than at the present time, keeping remembrance of any stirring event alive." – MBRN087

If what Webb Ellis did was notable, a stirring event, either as a good or a bad thing, it would surely have been recorded in Rugby School folklore as the 'Webb Ellis rule', or something similar. The fact that it was not throws doubt onto the authenticity of the Webb Ellis event.

IS THE WILLIAM WEBB ELLIS EVENT THE ORIGIN OF RUGBY UNION?

No it isn't. You don't need to be a rocket scientist to figure out that if Webb Ellis broke a rule then he must have been playing a game. What game was he playing? According to Matthew Bloxam, between 1813 and 1820 he was playing Football. So what game were they playing in 1845 when they wrote the first 'Football Rules'? The clue is in the name, they were playing Football. It's the game I've termed 'Football at Rugby School' to set it aside from other forms of football. It's the same game that evolved to be known as Rugby Union. Let's return to the consequences of the report and remind ourselves of the wording on the plaque:

THIS STONE
COMMEMORATES THE EXPLOIT OF
WILLIAM WEBB ELLIS
WHO WITH A FINE DISREGARD FOR THE RULES OF FOOTBALL
AS PLAYED IN HIS TIME
FIRST TOOK THE BALL IN HIS ARMS AND RAN WITH IT
THUS ORIGINATING THE DISTINCTIVE FEATURE OF
THE RUGBY GAME
A.D. 1823

Looking at what Wallace Reyburn says in his 1971 'A history of Rugby', he opens the book with:

"It is a popular misconception that during the course of a soccer match in 1823 a young fellow ran with the ball thus sowing the seed for a handling game which made a radical breakaway from the sport which was literally football. But in fact it was not as clear cut as that. What the Ellis boy did in 1823 at Rugby School was merely to add a new dimension to a handling game already in existence. The match in which the incident took place was certainly not soccer, since catching was allowed to any member of the team. There was, however, a restriction on running with the ball. This could only be done back from the mark at which the catch was taken; if the catcher wanted to go forward he could do so only as a follow-up to his kick ahead. The revolutionary thing that young Ellis did was to run forward with the ball in his hands." – WRHR001

Reyburn had the gist of it but then forgot about the origin and went on to write the rest of rugby history. Let's look closely at two sets of words on the plaque. To the layman it would seem that as Reyburn suggests above, a game of soccer was interrupted and spoiled by the upstart Ellis.

"... the rules of football as played in his time..."

"... distinctive feature of the Rugby game..."

When William Webb Ellis played the game it was called football, and by the time the plaque was placed in the school it was called Rugby Union Football. The sport of Football at Rugby School developed into the Rugby Union game as it was known in 1900 when the plaque was placed in Rugby School. To understand this development we need to follow the path of evolution for the sport; this is well documented in history so all that's required here is a simple outline of the major landmarks in the sport's history:

~1805 – Earliest accepted mention of Football at Rugby School (Macready's Reminiscences & Diaries)

1813 – Bloxam enters Rugby School and plays well organised football that has a set of verbally agreed rules (Football at Rugby School)

1823 – Ellis allegedly runs forward with the ball in a game that has a set of verbally agreed rules

~1830–40 – Running forward with the ball is allowed

1841 – "Running in" (scoring a try) is allowed

1845 – The first set of Football Rules are drawn up for Football at Rugby School.

1845–1862 – Old Rugbeians start to take the Football at Rugby School rule book to universities, other schools and into towns and cities where they form football clubs that play under the Football at Rugby School Rules. When the game was then played in locations other than at Rugby School, Football at Rugby School became known as football as played under the Rugby School Rules, or its condensed version, Rugby School Rules.

1862 – The Rugby School Rule book is widely distributed to clubs, universities and schools that are playing the game

1871 – Teams playing Rugby School Rules form a governing body to oversee the clubs involved. The new governing body is called the Rugby Football Union and a new set of rules, based on the Rugby School Rules, are drawn up by three Old Rugbeians (A. Rutter, E. C. Holmes and L. J. Maton). The sport of Rugby Union is created.

1886 – Rugby International Board formed

1890 – All international matches are to be played under the same rules

1895 – Breakaway of Northern Union clubs (creation of Rugby League)

1900 – Plaque placed in Rugby School

1930 – All teams to play under International Rugby Board rules, as opposed to under the rules of their nation's Union

2016 – The International Rugby Board is now known as World Rugby

As mentioned previously, the evolution of the game from that played at Rugby School to that played today is well documented, and as you can see from the above timeline, the same game was played by Matthew Bloxam, William Webb Ellis, Arthur Guillemard, Willie John McBride and Richie McCaw. The only thing that happened between the time of Matthew Bloxam and the present day Richie McCaw was that the game evolved somewhat, with minor changes to the laws being implemented here and there.

As the game went through its stages of development, the name changed from football (at Rugby School) to Rugby School Rules to Rugby Union. What's thrown a spanner into the working mind of the 20th & 21st century human being, that's you and I, is that the Association football game (soccer) that started in 1863 naturally assumed the term football, because it is played with the feet, and so we've grown up recognising football as being the round ball game. But if we cast our minds back to the first football history, George Routledge's 'A handbook of Football', we see that football was a very broad term, covering folk football, the school games (including Rugby School Rules) and Association football.

At Rugby School, Webb Ellis was playing football because that's what everybody called it back then. By 1900, however, the term football was generally used to refer to Association football only. In 1900, the Rugby Union game was the same game that was known as football in 1823. It had only evolved since Bloxam had entered Rugby School in 1813. The rules may have changed, but only through the natural evolution of a game being played by the same people, the pupils of Rugby School, at the same location – Rugby School. Therefore, William Webb Ellis did not invent Rugby Union. Which leads us to ask the question "what made us believe that he did?"

WHY DO WE THINK THAT WEBB ELLIS WAS PLAYING ASSOCIATION FOOTBALL?

It's back to the report of the Old Rugbeian Society where we find that there are three passages that mention Association football. The first mention is by the editor as he comments on Bloxam's information:

"In the passage just quoted another blow is given to Mr. Shearman's cherished theory, that Rugby preserved "the primitive game." We have already shewn that until 1749 Rugby was without any play-ground for football at all: and when the purchase of the manor-house and its enclosures supplied the deficiency, the game that was played (according to Mr. Bloxam's testimony) was not the game that Rugby knows now, but something more resembling Association Football." – ORSR009

The second is by Bloxam and it appears early in his 1880 article in the lead up to his description of the Webb Ellis event:

"In the latter half of 1823, some 57 years ago, originated, though without premeditation, that change in one of the rules which more than any other has since distinguished the Rugby school game from the Association Rules." – ORSR009

The third is again by the editor, commenting on the Webb Ellis story after receiving Thomas Harris' second letter:

"It may, we think, be fairly considered to be proved from the foregoing statements, that (1) in 1820 the form of football in vogue at Rugby was something approximating more closely to Association than to what is known as Rugby football to-day, (2) that at some date between 1820 and 1830 the innovation was introduced of running with the ball, (3) that this was in all probability done in the latter half of 1823 by Mr. W. Webb Ellis, who is credited by Mr Bloxam with the invention and whose 'unfair practices' were (according to Mr. Harris) the subject of general remark at the time." – ORSR022

So there are the three mentions of Association football and it must be noted that numbers 1 and 3 are meant to reflect what is said in number 2.

1 – "...but something more resembling Association Football."

2 – "...which more than any other has since distinguished the Rugby school game from the Association Rules."

3 – "... approximating more closely to Association than to what is known as Rugby football to-day..."

I may be being picky here, but to me number two (Bloxam) says that the sports are different and that handling is the biggest difference between the two, whereas numbers 1 and 3 (report editor) say that the games of Association football and Football at Rugby School were similar. It's an extremely clever and sophisticated ruse if number one was placed in front of number two to pre-suggest this and then number three was placed later on in the report to confirm what number one suggested. It certainly has the effect of making the reader believe that the two sports were similar. We can send the jury out on that one to decide whether it was done on purpose or not, but with three qualified barristers and a solicitor preparing the report, they have an extremely good way with words and it would be a difficult one to prove. So let's keep digging by asking a similar question:

WHY DO WE THINK THAT THE ORIGIN OF RUGBY UNION LIES WITH THE WEBB ELLIS EVENT?

Firstly let's look at the general outline of the report and its conclusions. The report is called 'The Origin of Rugby Football', which basically tells us that we are going to learn about the origin of rugby football if we read the report. From the second paragraph onwards it's telling us that Matthew Holbeche Bloxam identifies the origin of the sport as being the William Webb Ellis Event, and we must therefore believe that this is indeed the origin of the sport:

"...and also to enquire into the account of the origin of our game put forward on more than one occasion by the late Mr. Matthew Holbeche Bloxam..." – ORSR003

"We now come to Mr. Bloxam's account of the origin of the present Rugby game..." – ORSR009

"...that this was in all probability done in the latter half of 1823 by Mr. W. Webb Ellis, who is credited by Mr. Bloxam with the invention and whose 'unfair practices' were (according to Mr. Harris) the subject of general remark at the time." – ORSR022

The editor of the report is sure that Matthew Bloxam has pinpointed the origin of Rugby Union, but what did Matthew Bloxam actually say? The report includes Bloxam's 1880 Meteor article which was written in response to a letter to The Times and which mentions his 1876 letter to the Standard Newspaper, as well as his later article of the same year in the Meteor. Perhaps these last two accounts should have been included in the report, along with another mention of Ellis in 1883. We should take a look at them just to see what Bloxam says. But first it's worth noting that we are not alone in thinking that the report is a bit short of information. In WHD Rouse's book 'A History of Rugby School', published in 1898 just one year after publication of the report, he says of it:

"Several sources of information have not been used for this book, which would have greatly increased its value. Chief of these is the Books of the Big Side Levée." – WRRS262

Indeed others have pointed to the lack of readily available information, so let's go all the way back to the London Evening Standard letter of 1876. The Standard discussion is a chain of letters that originated from a small report about a football accident in which a young man named Ison died. Bloxam's letter is the last in the chain and this is what he says:

"Sir, - Permit an old Rugbeian, at school under the headmastership of Dr. Wooll, who resigned that office in the summer of 1828, to say a few words on the point in controversy in the present Rugby game. The running with the ball in one's hands is of no great antiquity as regards Rugby, it has there originated within the last half – century. It was not so during Dr. Wooll's mastership. When a boy had caught the ball in his hands he was not allowed to run forwards with it, but marking with the heel of his foot the spot where he had caught it, he was permitted without molestation to go back on his own side as far as he chose, the opposite side not being allowed to cross the point where the ball

had been caught. He who had caught the ball might then either punt it, or place it on the ground and kick it, or allow some one else on his side to kick it so placed; but directly the ball touched the ground, the opposite side might rush forward and contend.
Such was the rule of the game at Rugby School fifty years ago. MATTHEW HOLBECHE BLOXAM, at Rugby School from 1813 to 1821, and ever since a resident at Rugby.
Feb, 24." – LEVS18760226

In this letter Matthew Bloxam says nothing about Webb Ellis. It was 53 years after William Webb Ellis had supposedly invented a game that nobody yet knew he had invented.

Bloxam wrote the above letter in February 1876 and following that he wrote three major articles on Football at Rugby School (October 1876, December 1880 & November 1883). This is what he says in Meteor No 104 published on 10 October 1876.

The Meteor.
Edited by Members of Rugby School.
No. 104. RUGBY, October 10, 1876. Price 6d.

"FOOTBALL AND ATHLETICS
In the early part of the present year, some letters, written by old Rugbeians, about the present Rugby Football Game, appeared in the Standard, a well known London daily paper. In one of these letters the writer professed his belief that the Rugby School Football Game, at present played at Rugby, was of great and unknown antiquity. On this I wrote a letter, published in the Standard, to the effect that the present game, so far as the rules authorised the ball being taken up and carried by hand, the holder running with it, was unknown during the time I was at School, 1813 to 1821, and was I thought, introduced in Dr. Arnold's time. I have since ascertained that this change originated with a Town boy or Foundationer of the name of Ellis, William Webb Ellis, who was entered at Rugby School in 1817, and left at Midsummer 1825, being then elected as second exhibitioner of that year. It must, I think, have been in the second half year of

1824, that this change from the former system, in which the football was not allowed to be taken up and run with, commenced. At first the new practice did not succeed, but was soon set aside, and not again introduced, by whom I know not, till Dr. Arnold's mastership, 1828-42.
The game of Football was practised in this country before the middle of the 14th century. In 1349 it was, with other games, prohibited by authority, as interfering or supposing to interfere, with the practice of, and impending the progress of Archery.
In the early part of the 17th century it was discountenanced by James the First, who in his 'Basilicon Doron' says "From this Court I debarre all rough and violent exercises, as the football, meeter for lameing , than making able the users thereof."
It is, I think, owing the condemnation of the game by this Monarch, that we do not find it mentioned in the "Annalia Dubrentia," a collection of poetical effusions "upon the yearly celebration of Mr. Robert Dover's Olimpick Games upon "Cotswold Hills." These games, if not the origin, were the precursors of our present athletic sports. James the First gave them his sanction, and it may, I think, have been in compliment to him, that the game of football was omitted.
It continued, however, a game amongst countrymen in the 17th century, as appears from notice in the poems of Waller, born A.D 1605, died A.D. 1687:-

"As when a sort of lusty shepherds try
"Their force at Football; care of victory
"Makes them salute so rudely breast to breast
"That their encounter seems too rough for jest."

But an earlier poet, Barclay, in his "Ship of Fools," published A.D. 1508, treats of a game more resembling the present Rugby Football Game:-

"And now in the winter, when men kill the fat swine,
"They get the bladder and blow it great and thin,
"With many beans and peason put within:
"It ratleth, soundeth, and shineth clere and fayre,
"While it is throwen and cast up in the ayre,
"Eche one contendeth and hath a great delite
"With foote and with hands the bladder for to smite;
"If it fall to grounde, they lifte up agayne
"And this way to labour they count it nopayne,"

In conclusion, I may remark that the Rugby school footballs are well known all over the world..." – METR18761010

So in Bloxam's letter to the Standard earlier that year there is no mention of Ellis, but in the above article in the Meteor eight months later, he mentions Ellis for the first time. It is also of interest that in this first mention of Ellis the date given for the event is 1824, but in the book 'Rugby – The School and Neighbourhood', this has been changed to 1823 by the editor Rev W. W. Payne Smith, M.A.:

"...so far as the rules authorised the ball being taken up and carried by hand, the holder running with it, was unknown during the time I was at School, 1813 to 1821, and was I thought, introduced in Dr. Arnold's time. I have since ascertained that this change originated with a Town boy or Foundationer of the name of Ellis, William Webb Ellis...It must, I think, have been in the second half year of 1823, that this change from the former system, in which the football was not allowed to be taken up and run with, commenced. At first the new practice did not succeed, but was soon set aside, and not again introduced, by whom I know not, till Dr. Arnold's mastership, 1828-42." – MBRN110

In his article Bloxam states that there were rules when he played football 1813–1821 and that one of the rules has since changed. Then he gives us conflicting opinions. In one sentence he says that he thinks that this is when running with the ball started, and in the next sentence he says that it started but didn't succeed, and was then started again by an unknown person 5–19 years later. He then adds information about folk football but doesn't provide a link from folk football to Rugby School, only a similarity between the ball described in a 1508 poem and the Rugby School balls that are known worldwide. At no point does he say that Webb Ellis invented football or rugby; he just thinks that Webb Ellis started the change in one of the rules.

Back to the Old Rugbeian report. The one account that it relies on to attempt to prove that the Webb Ellis Event is the origin of Rugby Union is Matthew Bloxam's Meteor article dated 1880. This is what Bloxam says in that article:

"In the latter half of 1823, some 57 years ago, originated, though without premeditation, that change in one of the rules which more than any other has since distinguished the Rugby School game from the Association Rules." – ORSR009 / METR18801222

The important words in this paragraph are '*originated*' and '*change in one of the rules*', meaning that there is more than one rule, and that this is where the change in only one of those rules began. He does not say that this is the beginning of a new game. He does not say that Webb Ellis invented a game. He is saying that the game being played before and after the Webb Ellis event is the same game, but that one of the rules started to change. Ellis is playing an organized game with rules – Football at Rugby School. If he runs forward with ball, he is still playing Football at Rugby School, and the game remained as such until at least 1845 when the first rules were printed. Then, slowly as the game evolved and spread, it became football as played under Rugby School Rules, and then Rugby Union Football, and so on.

Let's look at the front cover and the title page of the first set of rules.

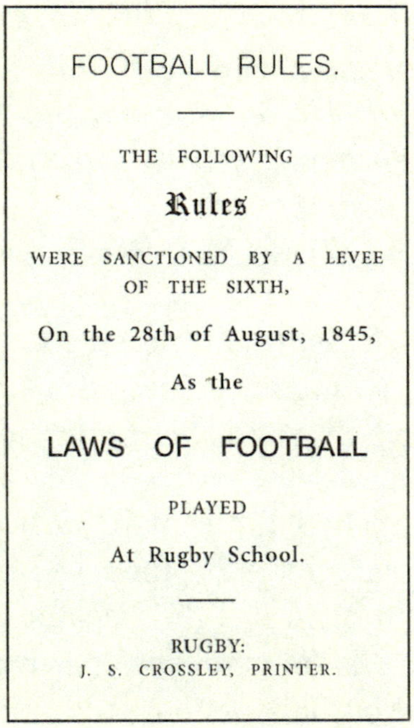
FOOTBALL RULES.

THE FOLLOWING

Rules

WERE SANCTIONED BY A LEVEE OF THE SIXTH,

On the 28th of August, 1845,

As the

LAWS OF FOOTBALL

PLAYED

At Rugby School.

RUGBY:
J. S. CROSSLEY, PRINTER.

Please note again on the front cover Football Rules 1845, the title page heading FOOTBALL RULES and The following Rules...... as the LAWS OF FOOTBALL. This is the same football that Mathew Holbeche Bloxam was playing in 1813, only the rules have evolved to include the action of running forward with the ball.

The final mention of Webb Ellis by Bloxam is in a paper that he read to the Natural History Society at Rugby School on 17 November 1883. The paper is published in the School Natural History Society Report for 1883:

"As to football, a different game was played to that at present; the rules were few and unwritten, but well understood. Two of the best players chose in a certain number on each side; the fags, all of whom were required to be present, unless specially excused by a Præpostor, were then divided in a rough and ready way, one half being sent to keep one goal, the other half the other goal. Any of the fags, who kept or were supposed to keep goal, might, however, follow up on that side by which their goal was defended, and this some of the juniors did, but at a respectful distance from the main body of the combatants, and as taking up the ball and running with it was not allowed, a kick at the ball was often obtained by a junior. The game was not then a scientific game; there were no matches to record, or press to record them. The taking up the ball first commenced in, I think, the year 1825, by a foundationer or town boy named Ellis; he was also a Praepostor. Had he not been of that grade in the school, he would, I think, have received more kicks than halfpence for breaking the rule. Backs and half-backs were unknown,

each combatant, subject to a few fixed rules, played as he individually might list. Whilst keeping goal and immediate attention was not required, games were often played by juniors, an old glove, stuffed with leaves, serving as a substitute for a football. There was no change of apparel for football, no caps, no flannels; hat and coat, or jacket, were simply doffed. There were no matches between house and house, or between the school and foreign teams. All were scratch games and unreported, yet the games were played with as much zest as at present, though when finished the game was no longer thought of." – MBRN074 / NHSR006

In his mention of Ellis, this time he's changed the date to 1825 and he still doesn't say that Webb Ellis invented a game. Bloxam seems to be unsure, his facts are all over the place, and I believe that he is beginning to doubt his source for the Webb Ellis story.

Summarising Bloxam's three major articles that include the Webb Ellis event, he first says that it took place in 1824, then 1823, and finally 1825. He is unsure as to whether it ever happened, but even if it did he states that Webb Ellis only started the change in one of the rules. There is no sentence in which Bloxam states that Webb Ellis invented the game of Rugby Football or that this is where the origin of Rugby Football or Rugby Union lies. He does say that this is where the change in one of the rules originated, and this is his only reference to the word 'origin'. As far as Bloxam is concerned, Webb Ellis was playing the same football that he played, which was also the same football that was played under Thomas Arnold 1828–1842 when the rules that allowed running forward with the ball commenced.

The Old Rugbeian report states:

"...the account of the origin of our game put forward on more than one occasion by the late Matthew Holbeche Bloxam..." – ORSR003

"We now come to Mr Bloxam's account of the origin of the present Rugby game..." – ORSR009

"...that this is in all probability done in the latter half of 1823 by Mr W Webb Ellis, who is credited by Mr Bloxam with the invention and whose unfair practices were (according to Mr Harris) the subject of general remark at the time." – ORSR022

Did you see anywhere in Matthew Bloxam's writings where he said that Webb Ellis had invented the game? I certainly didn't. There's a term for these types of statements – *'misinformation'* – 'false or inaccurate information, especially that which is deliberately intended to deceive', as defined by the Oxford online dictionary. And deceive it still does, with the governing body of Rugby Union, World Rugby, still promoting the Webb Ellis event as being the origin of the sport.

Webb-Ellis at Rugby, 1823

This illustration (from Wikipedia's Rugby School page) continues to perpetuate the misinformation. Note the Association football goals in the background. It is impossible for these to have been at Rugby School in 1823 because that game was not created until 1863.

SUMMARY – It is impossible for William Webb Ellis to have invented a game that he was already playing. The game that he was playing when he broke one of the rules was Football at Rugby School. Matthew Bloxam did not say that Webb Ellis invented the game; he said that he merely started the change in one of the rules. If Webb Ellis did catch the ball and run forward with it for the first time then he contributed to the evolution of the sport – the changing of actions, aims and rules. He did not invent Rugby Union. The report of the sub-committee of the Old Rugbeian Society has been proven to be biased towards naming the Webb Ellis Event as the origin. The report had no other purpose than to name Rugby School as the origin of the sport of Rugby Union. It is an extremely unsafe publication and the facts contained therein cannot be considered authentic unless they can be backed up by other independent sources.

CONCLUSION – The origin of Rugby Union is not the William Webb Ellis Event.

FOOTNOTE – There are many unanswered questions relating to the report but the aim of this book is to understand the origin of Rugby Union. We've proven that the William Webb Ellis Event is not the origin of Rugby Union and we've proven that folk football is not the origin either. So everything we've been told in the last 130 years, from Shearman onwards, is a load of bollocks. It's time to move on. What next? Once the Webb Ellis theory had largely become a myth, other historians moved back to the folk football theory, even though they were unable to provide links between folk football and Football at Rugby School. Not us, we're made of sterner stuff. We've proven that's almost certainly nonsense, so what we're going to do is to try and discover what the origin of the sport of Rugby Union really is.

Let's ask more questions. What does 'origin' mean? What is a sport? What is Rugby Union? But before we do that, this has been a really tough chapter for me to write and I need some self indulgence. If you can, go on Youtube and type 'Toy Dolls Nellie the Elephant' into the search engine. I love this song and the video in particular. The singer has such belief in himself, incredible confidence, he has 'attitude' in abundance and I want to be like him when I grow up. But before you go you have to promise me that you will come back and read this book to its conclusion. The next chapter is where the book starts to get interesting. Once you've listened to the sound of the Toy Dolls Nellie the Elephant please join me in singing this song to the same tune, or if you haven't listened to it you can use the normal Nellie the Elephant tune; the words work with both..........

Thank you, Thank you, Thank you..................

To Rugby School … William Webb Ellis went
He played a game of football and he created the Webb Ellis event
Seventy four years later, a group of Old Rugby's came
They twisted Matthew Bloxam's words
And said Ellis invented a game

Ooooooooooooooooooooooooooooooooooooooooohhhhhhhhhhh

Chorus

William Webb Ellis packed his trunk and said goodbye to folk football
Off he went with a puntabout punt, punt punt punt
William Webb Ellis packed his trunk and said goodbye to folk football
Off he went with a puntabout punt, punt punt punt

Nobody cared enough to find out the real truth
So it's down to me and you
We'll not be so uncouth

We've got to ask more questions
We've got to analyse some words
We've got to drag some memories up
And put them into words
Ooooooooooooooooooooooooooooooooooooooooohhhhhhhhhhh

Chorus etc.............

Enough, I can't cope anymore, let's get on........ let's go go go

CHAPTER 5 – ANALYSIS OF THE ORIGIN OF A SPORT

AIM – To understand what the word origin means in order to provide a set of rules that will govern and help us to identify where a sport's origins lie.

Some historians are seriously confused about the origin of Rugby Union. The following paragraphs are from Christopher Rowley's 'The Shared Origins of Football, Rugby and Association Football' published in 2015:

"Today there are seven codes – in alphabetical order – American football, association football, Australian rules football, Canadian football, Gaelic football, rugby league football, and rugby union football. They can be grouped in various ways...

...No matter which grouping is used, a basic fact remains: They are all descended from a common ancestor. The seven codes are a kind of demonstration of the power of evolution. Their remote ancestry, almost lost in the mists of time, involves developments in earlier civilizations that we barely know of or really understand." – CRSO0-intro-x

According to modern day author Christopher Rowley, Rugby Union, Association football, American football, Rugby League, Canadian football, Australian rules football and Gaelic football are all just different codes of football, and they all share the same origins. In looking at whether the origins of these seven codes of football are the same, I reach for my trusty Oxford Popular English Dictionary (2000 edition) to explore the definition of the word origin:

1. the point, source or cause from which a thing begins its existence
2. parentage, ancestry
3. (Math.) a point from which coordinates are measured [f. F or L origo (oriri rise)] – OPED564

I think it's safe to say that the first definition 'the point, source or cause from which a thing begins its existence' is what we are looking at, although the second definition 'parentage, ancestry' could raise a claim for the meaning.

Before we move on to sport, let's look at you – the origin of you.

Where do you begin your life's journey? Is it as a spermatozoon in your father's testicle, or as an ovum in your mother's ovary? A man's sperm and a woman's egg only carry 23 chromosomes of DNA each, so at those points you were only half a person. But when they joined together and made 46 chromosomes you became a single living being inside your mother. Then you grew into a foetus and finally you were born. So what is your origin? Is it when the sperm met the egg, or is it when you came out and they cut the cord? Most likely you regard the day you were born as being when you started your life. Even if you don't believe this, your government has decided that this is the date of your origin: on your official documents, passport and driving licence, you will find your date of birth, not your date of conception. Our date of birth is what we all celebrate because this for us is our origin – it is when we entered the world, separated from our birth parent and became a single entity. For sport it's similar. There's a point in time where each sport begins, where it becomes recognisable as that particular sport.

Just so that we are clear about where our personal origin lies, if you have mapped out your family tree, is the earliest date on that tree your origin? Mine is 1520 with William Snow born in Devon, but I know that William must have had parents and that my family tree stretches further back than that; we just don't have the information available. So I don't regard that as my personal origin, but I do recognise William Snow as an ancestor and acknowledge him as such. Even if I thought that William was my origin, it's possible that my great, great grandmother between us got too friendly with the milkman and that the Snow man she was married to was not my biological great, great grandfather – where would that leave me if I believed William Snow to be my origin? OK, back to sport.

Let's look at these sports again: Rugby Union, Association football, American football, Rugby League, Canadian football, Australian rules football and Gaelic football and ask ourselves "are their origins the same?" If the answer to that question is yes, then that means that they must be considered to be the same sport. Are they the same sport? No, they are not, they are similar. They are played on similar types of fields using a ball, but what separates these sports from each other are the differences in the type of field, equipment, aims and actions of the players, a set of rules that govern these actions and aims, and finally the governing body that oversees everything. They are seven different sports and for each of the above sports there is a point in time that defines when that sport became the distinct sport that it is today. Therefore, there are seven different origins, not one. Mr Christopher Rowley is incorrect in attributing their origins to be the same and so we should kick his opinion into touch and move on.

For the older more established sports, it's more difficult to pinpoint when in their existence they became recognizable as the sport that they are today. To be able to identify the point of origin, we need to understand sport in general. And to understand sport, we need to break it down into its various components and understand the differences between them. This we will do later on, but we first need to establish some ground rules for the terminology that we are going to use to describe the origin of a sport. We should look closer at the second meaning of 'origin' – 'parentage, ancestry'. On checking out parent and ancestor in the Oxpop (Oxford Popular English Dictionary), we find the following definitions that we will be able to use in relation to the origin of a sport:

parent – 5. A source from which other things are derived (OPED582)

ancestor – 2. An early type of animal plant or thing from which later ones have evolved (OPED024)

Let's look at how we can use 'parent' and 'ancestor' in relation to the origin of a sport. Rugby League's origins are well documented so that's an easy example to use. In 1895, the Northern Union was founded when several clubs broke away from the Rugby Football Union, which was the governing body for Rugby Union in England at the time. This is universally agreed as the birth of the sport of Rugby League. Therefore, we can say that Rugby League originated in 1895 and, because all the clubs that broke off used to belong to the Rugby Football Union, that its parent sport is Rugby Union. If Rugby Union is found to have a parent game or sport in the subsequent chapters, then that game or sport would be an ancestor of Rugby League. We have established our terminology in respect to the origin of a sport as:

Origin – the point in time at which a game/sport becomes identifiable as a single entity

Parent game/sport – the game/sport from which another game/sport has derived

Descendant game/sport – a game/sport that has evolved from another game/sport

Ancestor game/sport – a game/sport in the direct lineage of the game/sport in question

An addition I would like to make to the above list is:

Contributory game/sport – a game/sport that is not considered to be the parent sport but has either directly or indirectly influenced another game/sport.

This is where a sport can be determined to be a contributory factor to the birth of another sport. An example of this is triathlon, now an Olympic sport, which has the contributory sports of swimming, cycling and running.

I believe that I have identified two ways in which a sport can begin and these can be classified as follows:

CREATION – A game or sport is created when a group of people discuss and agree upon a course of action to create that new game/sport. For example, they could be playing one game and then decide upon a new course of action, like for the above mentioned Northern Union in 1895 that resulted in a group breakaway that eventually led to the sport of Rugby League. Triathlon is another created sport, originating in the

USA in 1974 when members of the San Diego Mission Bay Track club combined three contributory sports to make one race.

BIRTH – Can you remember the day you were born? I didn't think so. For most sports that started from scratch it's the same. We can't remember the day we were born because we have no memory retention at that age, but the reason a sport's origin isn't known is because it wasn't recorded at the time. People have DNA but the birth of a game or sport is mostly just a set of circumstances. A sport that has no parent sport or contributory sports can be considered as being 'born'. This is the most difficult type of sport for which to pinpoint an origin because in almost all cases no record of the birth exists. An example would be a running race. Who were the first two or more people to have a running race? This probably took place before man could write and so there was no record of the event. The first race may have been between two cavemen, one called Ug, the other called Og. Ug turned to Og and pointed at a rock 50 metres away and ran; Og didn't know why Ug was running but he thought he'd better get there first just in case. Og overtook Ug and won that first race and from then on the two raced to the rock after every hunting trip. Whoever ran in the first race, we will never know, but we do know that the first running race was run somewhere and at sometime prior to the formation of the first athletics club or organisation.

Now let's move on. To enable us to decide as to when a sport is created and when it is born, we need to decide what the components of a game or sport are and what exactly a game or sport is. Understanding the components of a game or sport is the key to determining where its origin lies. We need to combine the understanding of the mechanism of sport with historical information and references to view the bigger picture. So that we can dispense with ridiculous inventions and theories by people like Marshall & Shearman, if you are going to put forward a theory of origin like folk football or harpastum, then to make it acceptable you have to have an evolutionary path from the origin to the present day version of that sport.

SUMMARY – The word origin is quite clear in its meaning "the point, source or cause from which a thing begins its existence". We have used this meaning and other related words to form a set of terms relating to the origin of a sport. These terms will help us to pinpoint the origin of Rugby Union. We have postulated that there are two main ways in which a sport can begin: 1) creation, where a sport is decided upon by a group of people prior to it being played and 2) birth, when a sport begins owing to a set of circumstances.

CONCLUSION – We have identified a definitive meaning for the origin of a sport:

The origin of a game or sport is the point in time at which a game/sport becomes identifiable as a single entity. From that point onwards it must have an evolutionary path, drawn either theoretically or through the provision of evidence, to the modern day version of the sport in order for that point in time to be considered the origin.

FOOTNOTE – After the exertions of the last chapter I think we should tone things down and sing to the tune of 'happy birthday'

Happy terminology to me
Happy terminology to you
Happy terminology dear reader
Happy terminology to us

CHAPTER 6 – ANALYSES OF A GAME AND A SPORT

AIM – To define and understand what a game is and what a sport is; to identify the common components and the differences between the two and to look at the process of how a sport evolves.

Firstly we should decide what a game is and what a sport is. I reach for my trusty Oxpop and this is what it says:

Game: a form of play or sport, especially a competitive one organized with rules penalties etc. – OPED323

Sport: 1. an athletic (especially outdoor) activity; any game or pastime; an outdoor pastime such as hunting or fishing. 2. such activities or pastimes collectively; the world of sport; (in pl.) a meeting for competing in sports, especially athletics. – OPED800

There are other meanings to these words of course, but the meanings I am looking for are what we the sporting public believe the words stand for in relation to games and sports recognized as pastimes or professions, for example rugby, soccer, cricket, athletics, golf, monopoly, chess, darts, hide & seek, tag and so on. The above definitions are too general for my liking – I want something more specific. I put Google to the task of finding definitions for 'game' and 'sport', but I've failed to come up with anything either online or offline that's a generally agreed definition for either, so I'll write my own here based on what I perceive game and sport to mean:

GAME – a contest of luck and/or mental or physical skill between two or more parties under a common set of rules with the aim of determining a desired outcome or winner.

SPORT – a contest of physical skill, strength, speed, endurance, ability or physical artistic impression between two or more parties undertaken with a common set of laws set by a governing body with the aim of determining a desired outcome or winner.

We will talk more about the differences between games and sports later on. For the moment the above definitions are just to help us towards our understanding of what games and sports are. Our next step is to look closer at the make up of a game or a sport and to do this we should spend the night together, hypothetically of course. I know that it's the beginning of a chapter and we should be sensible but I feel a Rolling Stones song coming on........ Well maybe not, let's be serious again. But still......

LET'S SPEND THE NIGHT TOGETHER...... da da da da da da da da

Firstly picture your favourite large hall, preferably a sports centre that you've used a lot, or perhaps a school, college or university hall, a concert hall, or a big barn. Essentially it should be any indoor space in which you've taken part in a sport on a normal type of floor; things like ice rinks are not included. Thought of one? Can you place it in a time period that you're familiar with? For me I picture the Afan Lido in Port Talbot during the early 1980s. It's a very large, very high hall that's almost always split into two – one half for five-a-side football, the other half for badminton, trampolining and suchlike. I could talk all day long about this hall, about how one day I brushed shoulders with Arthur Scargill during the 1984 miners' strike. He was on his way to give a speech at a miners' rally and I was going the other way to play squash. I could talk about how I used to queue for hours for the trampoline, and the hundreds of games of badminton & five-a-side football I played there. I could go on forever, but this is not just about me, this is about you as well, it's about us.

Back to our night together; have you pictured your hall? Do you know where you are? You are going to need home advantage so you need to be sure of your hall, which I think we should now call the 'great hall', but if your hall has a special name feel free to call it that. It's an important place in your life, write it down here

………………………………………………………………………………….

Picture your hall and now picture a set of double doors that have magically appeared in the wall of the great hall. You open these doors and they open out into a room that's at least twice the size of your great hall. In this room is stored every type of sporting equipment known to man, so no matter what sport you want to play, the equipment is there in the room. There are even some race horses tucked away in the back just behind the Formula One cars. If you need this room to be four or ten times the size of your great hall then that's fine; we'll call this the 'equipment store room'. Look around and see how much stuff is in there, it's amazing. Now we need some helpers. I'm choosing the British & Irish Lions rugby team, with Sam Warburton as captain. You can pick whoever you want to be your helpers. Here's some space for you to name them if you want to

……………………………………………………………………………..

OK, this is where we are naughty. We are having a fun day doing whatever you do in your great hall, but we have agreed to hide away in the equipment store room and meet again in the great hall after closing. Five minutes until closing and you've hidden in the wooden gymnastics box – very original – but not as original as me because I pretended to be a speck of dust on a boxing ring canvas. It didn't quite work, but as nobody checked I got away with it, along with the British & Irish Lions rugby team who were acting as a group of slalom poles from a downhill ski run. The building in which your great hall lies has closed for the evening and all of the staff have gone home, but luckily for us they've left the lights on. I know that we shouldn't be doing this so please don't try it at home. I don't think it's breaking and entering, it's more hiding and playing, but I suspect it's against the law and you may get a criminal record if we are caught. But as we're here, let's play a series of sporting contests to decide who is the best sportsperson. It's me versus you, one on one, mano a mano or mano a womano, whichever suits you. Best of five sports. We'll adapt the rules of any sport to make it work for a one on one contest, we'll verbally agree on those rules and we won't cheat or argue about the rules or outcome of the contest once it has started. Agreed? Thank you. You get a point for every contest that you win and the first to three is the winner. Your helpers are there to help, put out equipment, towel you down when you're sweaty, bring on drinks *etc.*, but they are not allowed to help you play in any way, shape or form. This event is called the 'great hall all night sporting spectacular best of five one on one tournament' and we'll call it 'the spectacular' for short. It's got quite a ring to it, don't you think? I'm the reigning champion so I choose the first sport. We will play Association football.

Association football – I send the British & Irish Lions to get some goals and a football. First to three goals is the winner and you must be inside the goal area to score. I send George North to draw the goal area with some chalk. You start. GO. You dribble the ball along the wing, cut back inside, nutmeg me, cross into the area and score a goal. Sadly I can hear David Coleman's voice echoing in my head, 1-0. I can see that I've underestimated you so I put my game face on. If you turn back to Chapter 1, you'll see my game face in the right hand picture. I take the ball out and when I reach you I kick it against the wall into the space beyond you, control it nicely, dribble it into the area and slot the ball into the back of the net. YES. Richards is on form. You bring the ball out and attempt another nutmeg, but I read this one, rob you of the ball, take it into the area and slot goal number two. You bring it out again, feign a nutmeg, flick the ball over my outstretched foot, hurdle my swinging foot as I attempt to take your legs out from under you, dribble the ball into the area, shoot, but hit the post. The ball comes back at your feet and you make no mistake with the rebound and smash the ball into the back of the net. The score is now two all; the next goal wins it. I bring the ball out and attempt a side wall rebound move as per my first goal. You read this, intercept and dribble towards the goal, but just before you reach the area, I manage to get a toe to the ball and put you off your stride. You cut back and I harass you like a Jack Russell (the dog not the cricketer). My persistence eventually pays off and I win the ball back near my goal line. I point the air and shout, 'look at the flying pasty', you look, I kick the ball past you and run the ball the whole length of the pitch and score the goal. I win. I now lead 1-0 in the series. I hear David Coleman's voice again but this time it makes me a happy chappy.

Now it's your turn to choose a sport. Because you haven't played before, I'll show you how it's done. I'll choose bowls for you. I send off your support team to pick up the bowls mats, jack and sets of bowls. Your guys pass the British Lions in the store room as they are putting away the Association football goals; one or two jibes are directed at your support team from those rough rugby chaps, so I ask the Lions politely if they can refrain from intimidating your support team. Secretly I love what they have done and congratulate them when I am out of your earshot. It's not cheating, just unsportsmanlike. I'm not here to finish second, I'm a winner.

Indoor Bowls – You decide the rules and choose that the best of five ends wins it, with one point only per end. I fire the first jack because as the winner of the previous contest I get the choice of who starts first. My jack is long. I've played before but not regularly and not with any success either. My first bowl is off the carpet, yours is close to the jack. By the fourth bowl, you are lying three closest. The best I can do is to try and take the jack out. I miss, so you win the first end. You also take the second and despite me winning the third with a fluke bowl, you easily take the fourth end and win the contest with an end to spare.

One all. My turn to choose. I choose track cycling – individual pursuit, 100 miles – a new distance I've chosen especially for the evening. I send the Lions out for the portable velodrome tucked away in the back of the store room, just behind the race horses, and the carbon fibre bikes on the side. I knew they'd be a while fetching and assembling, so I've had a 20 minute snooze. I feel refreshed and ready to go.

Individual Pursuit – The track is just a touch less than 100 metres in circumference so the ends are quite tight and you fall off twice during the warm up. My confidence rockets but you've had enough practice and have gotten comfortable with the conditions so you decide on an all out attack to try and catch me from the start. I did have a game plan ready. I was thinking that I was just going to hunt you down for as long as it takes. Steady does it and eventually you tire and I make the catch. We start and you are out of the start gate like a rocket and before I know it you have caught me for 25 metres. On a track this small that means you've less than 25 metres to go to catch me and win. I wake up and put extra effort into getting back to the start position and I hold it there for 156 laps. You are starting to tire and slow down slightly and I do the same. I'm playing mind games with you now, I'm still fresh and I know I'm going to win but I want to keep you on the bike for as long as possible so that I tire you out for the two remaining sports. You keep slowing down more and I keep doing the same. Then you realise what I'm doing and after another 10 laps you decide it would be prudent just to get off the bike and concede, which you do.

Two points to me, one to you. It's your choice. Why don't you choose this time; pick a sport that you're good at, don't forget the rules and make sure that you give me a thrashing, otherwise the rest of this chapter will be a washout. Here's some space to write your victory into. It might be an idea to write it on the computer first, print it and paste it in – then all you have to do is publish it to our Facebook page and I'll add it to the website.

The score is two all; it's the decider. I can hear trumpets and a fanfare. It's just the British & Irish Lions and your support team improvising with their voices. Look at their grinning faces, silly boys (and maybe girls). To complete the spectacular it's a straight footrace. Running the length of the great hall – a sprint.

One Length Sprint – to start you must have at least one foot touching the wall and the winner is the first to touch the wall on the far side of the great hall. Ready, steady, GO. We are both out of the blocks fast. I'm getting slightly ahead. With only ten metres to go I'm about half a metre in front of you. I turn to grin in your face as I win the race but as I do so you stretch out an arm and touch the wall first. I time the finish poorly and run straight into the wall, before crumpling into a heap on the floor. Ouch. That hurt.

I've lost my title and you are now the spectacular champion. Congratulations. It's 8.45am and the great hall opens for its normal daily business at 9.00am, so we both instruct our support teams to clean up and tidy up after us. We have a final look around to make sure that everything is as it was when we started yesterday evening and we go back into the equipment store room and resume our hiding positions. 9.15am and the hall is busy enough for us to slip out. We wave goodbye to our support teams and head out into the big wide world – you a champion, me a loser. Well played. I was good once, let me tell you about it…

WHAT DO I KNOW ABOUT SPORT?

My earliest memory of taking part in a sport is when I was 7 years old and learning judo at the Afan Lido in Port Talbot under the tutelage of Alan Petherbridge M.B.E. (1964 Tokyo Olympic participant). From there I kept taking part in different sports before moving on to the next, starting with soccer, swimming, badminton, squash, cricket & rugby. When adulthood arrived and my body couldn't take any more rugby, I did soccer again, before taking up road running and athletics. I was the county 5000 metres athletics champion when I did my first triathlon in 1985 and one year later I started cyclo cross to help my triathlon cycle-to-run transition. Within three months I'd won my first cyclo cross race and gained my first international representative honours, cycling for Wales. I then went on to represent Wales at triathlon, mountain biking, mountain running, duathlon and marathon kayaking. The latter I combined with triathlon to win the veteran's category at the European Quadrathlon Championship in Berlin and I then became the World Champion for my age group in Prague a week later, August 2000. Other sports I've dabbled in include orienteering (Welsh short course champion), multi-sport (3rd place NZ Speight's Coast to Coast – 2 day event), table tennis, pool, darts, snooker, slalom kayaking, road cycling & rugby league, alongside others that I expect I've forgotten about. I managed the first UK college triathlon academy and have been responsible for starting several sports clubs and teams, including what was the largest triathlon club in Wales (I was chairman). I have also been a member of several club committees and was part of the local lottery funding committee. My full time job is running a sports memorabilia business, basically selling the history of sport, which I've done full time for the last 25 years, and my part time job is as a sports coach and personal trainer. Three of my children have represented Wales at sport and I've been involved with at least 8 different national squads. Understanding sport is a key factor to identifying the origin of a sport and I believe that I have the experience in sport that is necessary to undertake this job. I need to talk about myself a little more in this chapter and analyse instances in my own personal history, so please bear with me for a little longer as I draw on life's experiences and relate them to the analysis of sport in general. Whilst sport does have its serious side, it is mainly about having fun, enjoying good health and social interaction.

EXPERIENCE 1 – WEST STREET STORY

I have four children and my first two were girls, Laurie and Victoria. I used to take my two daughters to gymnastics in the West Street Gymnastics Centre in Gorseinon (Leigh Halfpenny country). There were two classes, one for the eldest (Laurie) and one for the youngest (Victoria). While Laurie did gymnastics, Victoria played in a 'safe soft play area', usually with the gym instructor's daughter, Non. In normal circumstances I'd take charge of such a situation and direct play for the two younger children. Victoria at the time was around three years old and Non was about six to eight months younger. I'd be looking to encourage positive play, getting the kids to do forward rolls or practise balancing, or I would try to teach them other useful skills.

Victoria and Non had other ideas, they ignored me and got on with their own thing. I had no problem with that because this pair pushed the limits of child's play to new levels and it was incredibly constructive play. In the area there were shapes, rings, sponge balls and safety matting; they would pick things up and throw them at each other, dodge them, run around and chase each other and then sit quietly and pass things back and forth between themselves, chatting and making up structured movements and rhythms as they went along. More often than not they'd work as a team, building things up and balancing on them and then knocking them down again before balancing more things.

I didn't need to do a thing, I was a redundant parent, and the play was so intense and fascinating to watch that I'm sure I could have sold tickets. At the time these two were toddlers and no-one had any idea what the future held for them. About 13 years later, in my role as Triathlon Academy Manager, I used to attend the local schools' cross country races and my female students were pitted against this incredibly driven and focused running machine called Non. When I saw her talking to her Mum one day, the aforementioned gym instructor, it suddenly clicked that she was little Non and I knew then why their play had been so special, it was the play of future champions. A few years later Non Stanford became the world triathlon champion and Victoria went on to become Welsh slalom kayaking champion; she also represented Great Britain and was a possible for the 2008 Beijing Olympics. She is now Dr Victoria with a PhD in Chemistry. The reason that I tell this story here is to show that even toddlers with a high level of intelligence have an aptitude for invention and play. Left alone they will adapt and improvise with anything that's available to them to have fun, altering their play to make it interesting and challenging for themselves.

EXPERIENCE 2 – THE ORIGIN OF THE FOLK FOOTBALL GAME AT BAGLAN PARK

This is a true story and it happened around 1972–1973. This story is about two boys, aged 12–13, one called Daio, the other called Parky – one is me and the other is Mark Harris, see if you can work out which one is which. Daio had a new rugby ball for Christmas and in January to March he kicked it around in the field of a school near to his house on his own. The Easter holidays arrived and he went out and called his mate Parky and they decided to go to the local park with the rugby ball for a kick around and to see if anyone else was in the park so that they could arrange a game. They were both keen to play rugby for the school and wanted to practise. They arrived at the park and there was no-one else there, so they commenced with a kick around, strung a few passes together, then kicked a little more, then strung a few more passes together and things got a little repetitive until one of the boys said 'see if you can stop me from touching the ball against that tree'. A wrestling match with the ball happened, the tree was eventually touched and the ball was kicked away into the distance so that they could try it again; and so the Baglan Park Folk Football game was born.

There were unwritten verbal rules, the one that had last touched the tree with the ball would have to kick the ball at least five metres away from the tree in a direction nominated by the opposing player to start the next round. The aim of the game was to gather the ball and touch the tree. There were no other rules, the boys could be wrestling each other for the ball for 20 minutes at a time, things were relatively even, but a pattern of play developed. If Parky touched the tree he'd make a shorter kick, Daio would gather the ball but Parky would catch him straight away, eventually rip the ball off him and score. Then Daio learnt not to pick the ball up straight away but to kick it again and then pick it up once he was out of reach of Parky. Daio was a great dodger so if there was room he'd dodge around Parky and score. Parky learnt to stay near the tree because he could nearly always catch Daio when he approached the tree. Stand offs and running around trees could last 10–15 minutes and Parky would never fall for the 'look at that flying pasty' trick like you did. The wrestle for the ball could last another 20 minutes. One thing was certain: the boys would get absolutely plastered in mud. Daio's mam, sick of washing muddy clothes, called an end to Baglan Folk Football after about two weeks by banning him from going to the park and getting dirty.

Let's look at these two experiences more closely. Victoria and Non were playing, but there was an aim to their play and actions. Their communication skills and understanding were limited, basically because they were not old enough to hold a conversation, so they were too young to develop rules and so no game appeared out of their play. Daio & Parky on the other hand understood the game of rugby but knew that they could not play a proper rugby match because there were only two of them, so they started with actions, then developed an aim and created a set of rules to channel those actions in order to benefit their overall objective, which was to improve their rugby skills. These are the building blocks of sport. Let's analyse this in more detail.

To start with we are going to look at the common denominators that make up all games and sports. Each game or sport is made up of the following six ingredients, components or elements:

Location, personnel, equipment, actions, aims and rules.

Let's define each of these ingredients and let's look back at the spectacular to see how the sporting contests that we played relate to these 6 ingredients.

GAMES & SPORTS INGREDIENT LIST

LOCATION – This is where the game or sport will take place; a location can include fixed objects such as buildings, trees and other unavoidable factors such as water.

Among others a location could be a field (cricket, soccer, *etc.*), court (tennis, basketball, *etc.*), water (swimming, diving, yachting, *etc.*), mountain (skiing, bobsleigh, orienteering, *etc.*) or road (running, cycling, *etc.*). Other permanent fixtures of a game/sport that must be present at the location and that aren't supposed to move, or are meant to be avoided during play, are also included in this ingredient – e.g. a tennis net, rugby posts, soccer goals or slalom poles.

The spectacular; step 1 – The spectacular location was the great hall. In your mind clear the great hall so that there is no-one in it. That's our location. Then add the Association football goals, bowls carpet and velodrome, plus any permanent fixtures from the sport that you chose.

PERSONNEL – The people and/or animals that are at the location and that are going to play and/or judge the game/sport.

The spectacular; step 2 – The spectacular personnel were you and I. When we walked into the great hall we joined with the location to make up the first two ingredients.

EQUIPMENT – The moveable objects; things that are controlled by the players and are used during the game/sport. These may already be at the location or can be brought by the personnel. Equipment, however, is not a necessity and a game/sport can take place without this component. A player's dress or equipment that is worn or fixed to the person throughout the duration of the game/sport does not count here, for example boxing gloves, swimming goggles, running shoes, skis, ski poles, or tennis, badminton and squash racquets. These items can be considered under personnel because they are a fixed part of the participant's dress/equipment and they are necessary in order to take part in the game/sport. Equipment can be deemed to be balls, arrows, shuttlecocks, darts, pucks, javelins, discus, *etc.*, *i.e.* items that require an action to be exerted upon them in order to make them a part of the game/sport.

The spectacular; step 3 – That's why we had our support team. In Association football the equipment was the ball. In bowls, it was the jack and bowls. We didn't have any equipment in individual pursuit as the bikes were personnel, and we didn't use any for the one length sprint either. You need to work out whether we used any equipment in your sport so I'll leave a space for you below to enter this if applicable.

ACTIONS – There needs to be movement or interaction between the above three or the first two. This can include all types of movement, such as running, kicking, hitting, paddling, throwing, dancing, driving, shooting, jumping, dribbling with a ball, *etc.*

The spectacular; step 4 – Running, dribbling, shooting a ball, tackling, shooting bowls, riding a bike, (your sport)...and running.

AIMS – There needs to be an aim to each action – e.g. passing a ball to a player in a better position, hitting a shuttlecock to put your opponent in a difficult position, bowling a ball to try and get your opponent out. There also needs to be an overall objective or main aim to the actions – e.g. to score a goal, force an error, hit a winner, run the fastest, avoid the poles, *etc.*

The spectacular; step 5 – To score 3 goals, to win 3 ends, to catch the other rider, , to reach the wall first

RULES – A set of rules needs to be created in order to determine how the actions and aims define the contest – e.g. you can't pass forward, if you hit a pole you lose points, the first to the finish line is the winner, you mustn't punch an opponent, the contest ends after 60 minutes, *etc.*

The spectacular; step 6 – Association football adapted rules, Bowls adapted rules, Cycling adapted rules, (your sport)... adapted rules and Athletics adapted rules.

The above six ingredients constitute a game or sport and each game or sport needs a name so that we can easily differentiate it from other contests. Let's look at some more examples as to how these ingredients relate to some of the sports that are played today. These examples are only intended to provide a general idea and do not comprehensively list all aspects of each ingredient.

Location	Personnel	Equipment	Action	Aim	Rules	Name
50 metre swimming pool, timing mechanism	1 swimmer per lane		Swim butterfly	To swim as fast as possible over 2 lengths	Set by world governing body	100 metres butterfly race
Golf course	Golfers & golf clubs *etc.*	Golf balls	Swing club to hit ball *etc.*	To get the ball inside the hole in as few strokes as possible	Set by world governing body	Golf
Badminton court, net	2 players & racquets	Shuttlecock	Hit shuttlecock with racquet	To force opponent into error or to play a winning shot	Set by world governing body	Badminton singles
Boxing ring	2 boxers & boxing gloves		Punching	To knock out or outscore	Set by world governing	Boxing

				your opponent	body	
Road	Runners		Running	To run 26.2 miles as fast as possible or to survive	Set by world governing body	Marathon race
Association football pitch	22 players plus officials	Football	Kick & head ball, pass or dribble ball, handle ball (goalkeeper only)	To kick the ball into the opponent's goal and to score more goals than them	Set by world governing body	Association football match
Water, road	Triathletes		Swimming, cycling, running & transitioning	Swimming 2.4 miles, cycling 112 miles & running 26.2 miles as fast as possible, or to complete the course, depending on personal goals	Set by world governing body	Ironman Triathlon
Table tennis table	4 players & bats	Ball	Hit ball with bat (alternate players)	To force opponent into error or to play a winning shot	Set by world governing body	Table tennis (doubles)

Now let's look at Baglan Park Folk Football:

Location – Baglan Park & tree

Personnel – Daio & Parky

Equipment – Rugby ball

Action – Running, kicking, tackling and wrestling with the ball

Aim – To touch the ball against the tree

Rules – The person touching the tree has to kick the ball at least five metres away from the tree to start the next round and in the direction nominated by the opposing player.

Name – We didn't get that far so I've given it a historical name, Baglan Park Folk Football.

My childhood was littered with such examples of made up or adapted games, particularly during my early years of comprehensive school.

EXPERIENCE 3 – SOMETIMES I WENT TO SCHOOL

When I was at my first comprehensive school, Glanafan, there was an apparatus that consisted of two sets of A bars with an adjoining top bar. I arrived at the school in the blue Llynfi double decker bus to discover that this game was already in existence and I was keen to play. There were no written rules but the aim of the game was to cross from your side of the bars to the other side. An opponent lined up on the other side. There was no time limit and no-one kept score. There were three ways of crossing over: by going down (where you swung across like a monkey), by going up (where you shuffled across with a leg over the top bar) and by going through the middle (where you put one elbow over the cross bar). You lined up on the bars and faced your opponent, agreeing with him before hand which method was to be used for battle and then you had to knock your opponent off the bars and try to get to the other side before another boy launched himself onto the bar. I don't remember any girls playing this game, most likely because the only choice of uniform they had was a skirt.

There were tactics involved in this game just like any other – you weighed up your opponent and if you knew his strengths you'd call his weakness. If you disagreed and took too long, the older boys in the queue behind you would get restless and push you on whether you were ready or not. I always chose to go up – my upper body was weak and my legs were strong so I used to cling on to the bar and kick like hell to get to the other side. If you had Cookie behind you, you would always let him go first because if two were fighting on the bars in front of him he'd always launch himself off the bar and clip you with his feet just above the waist, which hurt like hell. He was the Webb Ellis of our playground.

Location – Glanafan, fixed bars in the playground

Personnel – Two teams of an indeterminate number

Equipment – None needed

Action – Swing or shuffle across bars

Aim – To get to the other side

Rules – Cross using one of three ways – up, down or middle – to be agreed with your opponent

Name – We just called it 'the bars'

I used to play the bars every playtime and lunchtime until the blisters on my hands got too painful. Then it was off to the dab wall – a wall about five metres across with a distinctive red brick line at the height of about 1.5 metres and a drainpipe smack bang in the centre of the wall. The aim of the game was to throw a tennis ball at the wall so that it would hit above the red brick line. The next player had to catch the ball before it bounced four times, otherwise they were eliminated. If a player caught the ball on the full then the thrower was out. We'd usually start with around eight players and the last player won a point. Then we'd start again. Hitting the drainpipe was the key to this game as the ball would more often than not come off at an angle and increase the difficulty for the next player. I would stick at this game until my throwing shoulder got too sore and then head back to the bars.

Location – Glanafan, wall, drainpipe

Personnel – Any number of individual players

Equipment – Tennis ball

Action – Catch and throw the ball

Aim – To get the next player out

Rules – Four bounces maximum, ball thrown above the line, if caught on the full you're out

Name – Dab

At lunchtime we would occasionally play Mob (name changed to avoid religious repercussions). The Velindre estate was the field of play. You weren't allowed out of the estate and the school was out of bounds. Two chasers were picked and the rest were runners; the aim of the game was for the chasers to catch the runners, tap them on the head and say 1-2-3-Mob. That runner then became another chaser and the game ended when everyone was caught. We'd usually play with about 50–100 of us and not once did we finish the game.

Location – Velindre Estate

Personnel – Any number of kids

Equipment – None

Action – Running, dodging, chasing and tapping of heads

Aim – To catch others or not to get caught

Rules – Stay in the estate, the school was out of bounds, tap on the head 1-2-3-Mob

Name – Mob

The above three games played at Glanafan are classic examples of games that have evolved through the ingenuity of children. Mob was most likely a game that scouts played and there were probably written rules somewhere, the same for dab but we played this against any wall with any ball except a cricket one. The bars were probably unique and could have been a game developed specifically by the past pupils of Glanafan. There was a lot more going on in my school yard but those were the ones that I played. What defines these games is the location, the personnel, the equipment available, the action, the aim, the rules and the name. It's not that anyone sat down and thought these things up and committed them to paper before starting the game, we just got on with playing these games. There is one certain element to them though, they each must have started somewhere and evolved into the form of the game that I played.

EXPERIENCE 4 – PAPER CLIP OLYMPICS

So what are the 'paper clip Olympics', I hear you ask. It's a collection of made-up games that are each invented using only the materials available in any given location. Back in the early 1980s my friend Bryan 'Charlie' Cokely and I used to train at soccer together on a local sports field. On the walk to training, to keep ourselves entertained we would challenge each other to make up games from the materials available, which was mostly litter. We invented some really bizarre games and we became so proficient at engineering a contest, we'd boast 'give us a paper clip and a piece of paper and we'll invent an Olympic sport out of it'. So when we invented these different games we'd call them 'paper clip olympic sports'. Then Charlie moved to Australia and went on to a professional soccer career with Sydney City and Woollongong Wolves. I've since carried on inventing silly games and have subjected my family to numerous 'paper clip olympic sports'. We have what we call 'the bag of tricks', which is full of balls, bats, racquets, frisbees and other throwing things. We've taken this bag to the beach and on holidays and we use the equipment inside to create games to play. At the beach we play a made-up game called 'gate rounders' and the old favourite, dab. We draw circles in the sand and aim Frisbees and balls in the circles – nearest to the centre wins.

Family & friends prior to the 2016 Gate Rounders World Championship Series on Aberavon Beach with the 'the bag of tricks' in the foreground

At different beaches we play different games, the location always dictating what we play. When we are in the countryside we play other games like Melon Boat Racing (where we each design a boat made out of melon rind and sticks and race them down the river) and Best Fallers (competing for the most dramatic and realistic fake fall down a large hill).

I used to coach a swim lane in the mornings in Neath. There was the serious training – we were the first team home in the first ever British Aquathlon Championships (swimming & running race) – but every Friday we'd finish early and play made-up games. I didn't invent them all, we worked as a team, tried things out, discussed what worked and developed the games that we played. These included underwater walking and float balancing. Everything we played was dictated by the personnel, location & equipment. We developed them further with aims and rules and lastly we gave them a name. In underwater walking, you had to walk on the floor of the pool to the other end. There were unwritten rules: you had to keep at least one foot on the floor at all times. In float balancing you had to stand on a kickboard/float and try to place another one under your feet. If your foot touched the floor of the swimming pool you were out. The person with the most kickboards under them was the winner.

Every game or sport must take place in a location and the nature of the location and the equipment available typically dictate the type of contest . Lastly, please bear with me, it's my book and I want to include this one. What type of game or sport would you expect to find taking place at a rugby club?

EXPERIENCE 5 – TOUCHY NOSEY

After the 2015 'Aberavon Green Stars Rugby Club Annual Round the Pier Swim', I was socializing in the clubhouse with my triathlon mates Martyn Powell, Chris Price, Nathan Rees, Huw Pascoe & Steve Wilkinson. Martyn now coaches the Neath pool early morning swim session that I mentioned previously and the conversation moved on to the Friday morning games. Someone asked as to how we decided what games we should do and how they come about. I can't remember my full answer because I'd had a few too many Guinnesses, but to show the boys how easy it was to invent a game we invented one there and then.

Location – Aberavon Green Stars RFC clubhouse – patch of grass outside (near the queue for the burgers)

Personnel – Those previously mentioned – 6 individual players including myself

Equipment – Pint of beer (lager optional) in a glass

Action – To touch your nose with the glass

Aim – To do it as artistically as possible

Rules – You must lift the glass from a position at least below hip level to touch your nose in the most artistic way, with the result of the contest to be decided by a general consensus of opinion by those competing

Name – I put the naming of the game on to Huw Pascoe who called it 'Touchy Nosey'

The game commenced and I was disqualified in the first round because I forgot to touch my nose with my glass. It is now on record that the first official joint Touchy Nosey World Champions are Huw Pascoe and Chris Price. Pricey was a natural and I'm tipping him to go on to greater things in the future – possibly the first Touchy Nosey professional.

Three of the original Touchy Nosey contestants, Martyn Powell, Chris Price & myself

The TV series 'It's a Knockout' or 'Jeux Sans Frontières' is a classic example of game invention. Every week a series of bizarre new active games were invented for the benefit of a European TV audience. Each game was made up of the six ingredients: location (TV set), personnel (competing teams), equipment (various), actions, aims and rules, and each was given a name. Invent a game yourself. If you are in the office, in the lounge or in the kitchen, pick up something light and manœuvrable – a pen, cushion or spoon. Throw it at something immovable, a desk or a chair, or into a saucepan. Try to get it in the centre or as close to the edge as possible; make a mark where it landed with something like a paper clip or a penny piece. Challenge someone else to get it closer. Then add variations – land it at an angle, or do as many as you can in 30 seconds while hopping on one leg with a finger in your ear. Grab more people, split into teams, spell out the person on your left's name backwards while you are playing. Add rules as you go along and if you have fun, you'll play again and again and develop the game further and then invent some more. It's so easy to invent a game.

None of the made-up games in my experiences, either that I have invented or been involved with, will become Olympic or professional sports, they are just examples of how easy it is to invent a game. I've never woken up in the morning and said to myself 'I'm going to invent a new game today'. The games I've made up just happened; it's human nature to be competitive, to be artistic, to be inventive and to have fun. Fun is a key element to new games; it's what brings players back to them. When you experience something good, the chemical dopamine is released into the brain and the brain is rewarded with a natural high. Other chemicals like endorphins, oxytocin and serotonin are released too and human nature dictates that if you do something and it makes you feel good, you will do it again and again. That's why games and sports are so great, even if you are not a natural winner, there are so many different opportunities to release those chemicals and reach those highs; you meet new people, you accomplish new goals and you try out new things. Throw a balloon into a room full of people of any age and watch what happens. A game of 'keep the balloon up' immediately starts. Most people will join in and every time someone hits the balloon into the air, chemicals are released into their brain as it registers a success. The smiles on the faces of the players are the proof that it's fun.

Join me to see how we can develop this into a full blown international sport. We've thrown a balloon into a room full of people sitting on chairs, picture a school assembly or a theatre audience for example, and they immediately hit the balloon into the air – we have a location, a room, we have personnel, the people in the room, we have equipment, a balloon, we have an action, hitting the balloon, we have an aim, keeping the balloon in the air. Do we have a game? No, what we have is play. No-one is keeping score because there are no rules. Split the room in half and draw a line down the middle, with half of the people on side A and half on side B. We tell both teams that they have to knock the balloon into the other half of the room and that the team that has the balloon in their half for the least amount of time is the winner. We both have a stopwatch; I'm timing side A and you're timing side B. We start our watches when the balloon crosses the line and enters our side and we stop it when the balloon crosses the line on the way back to the other side. We now have a rule and we have a game, so let's give it a name. I think we'll call it 'booonce' (the emphasis is on the 'ooo', it actually sounds like seven or eight 'o's, like booooooooonce).

Good, now that we've got the name straight, the people in the room get on with playing the game. Because they are so close to the line, they hit each other instead of the balloon and so we spread the chairs apart or vacate a couple of rows if they're fixed, and draw a two metre wide corridor between the two teams with a piece of chalk. They seem to be having more fun when the balloon is in the air for longer between hits, so to keep the balloon up higher for longer we introduce a net in the middle, which leads to more smiles and more happiness. At the end of the contest, your partner and kids were in the winning team and they had FUN, so when you all got home they posted videos on Facebook and Youtube. Friends and other people clicked on the videos and saw how much fun they were all having and asked as to how the game was played. Your partner wrote the rules down on Facebook.

Six months later your local supermarket has sold out of balloons because the local schools, scout and guide groups, churches and even pubs have started playing booonce. A local league is formed in your town and within two years the whole of the UK is playing. Some teams and leagues have changed the rules to suit their playing area so several teams get together to form the UK Booonce Association to regulate play. This covers the game in the UK, which is now booming more than ever, and teams are coming over from Europe to play. The Deutsche Booonce Federation has slightly different rules so a meeting between all of the booonce playing countries is called and the International Booonce Union is born. Taylor Swift includes a game of booonce in her latest music video and it has a trillion hits on Youtube. Participation in the game increases ten fold and within six years nearly every country in the world has its own booonce federation. The sport is applying for Olympic recognition and you've never played the game because you are still holding the stopwatch. Your partner and kids are international celebrities with their own trading card sets and merchandise deals. Well, someone has to make sacrifices, and don't forget I'm holding the other watch, I've made sacrifices too. On the bright side at least your watch still works.

Let's look at the evolution of the game 'booonce' from its birth to becoming an international sport. 0 means that we have nothing.

1. Location = 0

2. Location + personnel = 0

3. Location + personnel + equipment = 0

4. Location + personnel + equipment + action = play

5. Location + personnel + equipment + action + aim = play

6. Location + personnel + equipment + action + aim + verbal rules = game

7. Location + personnel + equipment + action + aim + written rules = organized game

8. Location + personnel + equipment + action + aim + written rules + governing body = sport

9. Location + personnel + equipment + action + aim + written rules + national governing body = national sport

10. Location + personnel + equipment + action + aim + written rules + world governing body = international sport

Looking at the above equations I think it's safe to say that a game is born at step 6 and a sport at step 8. The above 10 phases can be split into three distinct groups.

Group 1 (1–3) – Physical basics – The location, people and equipment are physical entities, they are tangible; we can reach out and touch them.

Group 2 (4–6) – Variants – The actions, aims and verbal rules. They are variable and when changed they will usually help a sport to evolve and will enhance the playing experience of the participants. These are the three main ingredients of a game or sport and are what makes each individual sport unique. Actions, aims and verbal rules are not physical entities and unless they are recorded they will only exist in the memories of the players or spectators.

Group 3 (7–10) – Organisation – This is where a sport gets serious, the rules are written down and governing bodies are formed.

Think back to the spectacular. What if you chose handball but your support team couldn't find the handball goals or ball? You sent them back in and they turned up with the Association football goals and ball. They took forever just to do that, so rather than send them back in again we used the Association football equipment and improvised in order to play handball. We could do this because they are similar and with our adapted equipment and our one on one rules we could play a full game of one on one handball. Let's look at how things changed with respect to the six ingredients compared to when we were actually playing Association football. Group 1, there's no change in the physical basics. We are in the same location, we are the same people and we used the same equipment. In group 2 we see changes. Different actions – we are throwing the ball instead of kicking it – different aims – the aim is now to throw the ball into the net to score a goal and different rules, which we would have adapted and changed from team handball. In this instance the differences between the sports of Association football and handball are all found within group 2 of the ingredients. Group 1 remains unchanged and group 3 is irrelevant.

THE BEGINNING OF A SPORT

Let's return to Shearman and Marshall, who I believe were attempting to imitate Charles Darwin's Origin of the Species. The evolution of a sport is not like Darwin's theories; the evolution of man is a serious business. In our evolution, something has to exist before something else can – DNA (46 chromosomes) – and we can trace ours back in time. The evolution of a game or sport is not like that of man, there are no fossils of the ancient games that used to exist, you can't go digging up a goal scored in folk football games like harpastum or cnappan. You can dig up the people who played it, and possibly some of the equipment that was used if it hasn't perished (group 1) and the rules may even be written down somewhere (group 3), but the game itself, its variants, the aims and actions of the players and the verbal rules (group 2) no longer exist.

That's one of the reasons why we spent the night together. We checked after we had finished the games that everything was the same as it was before we started playing. Group 1 of the above list did not change because nothing got broken and group 2 no longer exists because the ingredients in that group only belong in the present. However, because we've written about the spectacular it now exists in a historical context, but if we hadn't have written about it the memory of it would eventually have faded away and when we're both pushing up the daisies there would have been no recollection of this information. That's why it is so difficult to pinpoint the origins of a sport that is born, because at the time, the people playing it did not record their efforts.

Earlier on we decided that the origin of a game or sport is the point at which it becomes a single entity. How can we relate this to our two forms of origin: creation and birth?

CREATION – A game/sport that has a parent or contributory game/sport can only find its origin by creation if the contributory game/sport has reached at least stage 6 of the above progression. Rugby League was born at stage 9 of its parent sport's progression and triathlon was born at stage 10 of its three contributory sports' progressions.

BIRTH – This is harder to define. Arguably it could be at stage 6 when it becomes a recognizable game but I believe it may be possible that it could be at stage 5 when an aim is introduced. Booonce was certainly only recognizable when it had reached stage six but I think that this is a definite grey area that needs to be explored in greater detail.

EVOLUTION OF A SPORT

We have decided that a game/sport is made up of six ingredients and as a rule these never stay the same from the beginning of when a game/sport is first played to how it is played today. The people who play and organize games and sport are always looking for a greater or a safer experience to enhance its appeal and to keep the participants interested. So how and why does a game/sport evolve? There are two major reasons as to why:

1. To solve any problems that occur.

2. To take opportunities to enhance the game/sport wherever possible.

Changes in rules will usually be made to cater for one of the above. In the sport booonce we introduced the two metre gap between the teams to solve the problem of players hitting each other and we then introduced the net to enhance the game for the players. Sports are evolving constantly. The sport of Rugby Union has seen many changes in the laws relating to the scrum, in particular the binding of prop forwards. These have mostly been changed for safety reasons. The collapsing of a scrum can lead to neck injuries for players and these laws are attempting to solve that problem. The tip tackle law is another that has attempted to solve the problem of too many injuries. The law that allowed players to throw a line-out ball further back than the actual exit point where the ball went into touch was an enhancement to the game. Players can now restart the game themselves or throw the ball to a team mate, speeding up the game and introducing running in broken play, which is a much greater spectacle for players and spectators alike. If you are not familiar with the sport of Rugby Union, then look to your own sport and ask yourself the following two questions in relation to a law change:

1. Did the change solve a problem?

2. Did it make the sport better?

If you can't answer yes to one or both of the above questions then you need to select other lawmakers to the governing body of your sport.

If you've gotten to this point and you are scratching your head and thinking 'what is this bloke on about?' Or you've read through and nothing has seemed remotely interesting, then you need to get practical. I bet you skipped the 'invent a game now' opportunity. It's redemption time. Don't move on until you've invented a game. Go to the shop and buy some balloons, blow them up, clear your mind and focus on the balloons, focus on the actions that you can do with them and make up some aims; relax and focus. If you can't find balloons then go to the bathroom or kitchen and use sponges instead, or cushions. It's always best to use something soft when you are creating a game, trust me on that one – I learnt the 'hard' way. Focus on actions and aims first and then create a rule. You've invented a game, now let's move on.

SUMMARY – We now have definitions of what play is and what games and sports are and we know when play becomes a game, and when a game becomes a sport. We have decided that there are six common ingredients to every game and sport: location, personnel, equipment (optional), actions, aims and rules. Everything within a game/sport fits into one of these categories. It is very easy to invent a game by combining these six ingredients. An international sport that is born has a progression of ten steps that can be used to identify the status of the sport along its line of evolution. There are three distinct groupings along this pathway: physical basics, variants and organisation. The origin of a game/sport that is born would most likely be identifiable as being the point at which it reaches step 5 (introduction of an aim) or step 6 (addition of a rule). A game/sport will continue to evolve, as driven by the need or want to solve problems or enhance the playing experience.

CONCLUSION – It is very easy to invent a game and there are common denominators in games and sports that can be used to help identify the origin of a sport.

FOOTNOTE – Now that we have a set of common components for a game/sport and a set of definitions & rules that govern the origin of a game/sport, we can look at the origin of Rugby Union and decide where this lies. To the tune of Elvis' 'Blue Suede Shoes'…

It's one for the location
Two for who you know
Three for the equipment
Let's go go go……………..
But don't you
call it a game without rules
A ha haaaa

You can call it anything
But it's not a game without rules
A ha haaaa

CHAPTER 7 – ANALYSIS OF RUGBY UNION

AIM – To analyse the evolution of the six ingredients of the sport of Rugby Union to see if we can find any clues that can help us to define the origin of the sport. To double check this analysis against the previously held theories – that the origin of Rugby Union lies with either folk football or the William Webb Ellis event.

In Chapter 3, we traced Rugby Union back to the game of Football as played at Rugby School in 1803–1806, but all we have from that time is just a mention of football. The earliest point on our timeline when we are provided with details relating to the laws, actions and aims of the game is in the memories of Matthew Bloxam. We then have correspondence from the former pupils who attended the school in the 1830s, contained within the 1897 Old Rugbeian Society report, and then in 1845 we have the first published set of rules. The progression from then on is reasonably simple to follow, through the rule books themselves and publications such as 'The History of the Laws of Rugby Football' by Admiral Sir Percy Royds. It is unfortunate, however, that the good Admiral believed in Marshall's folk football theory and that several references to folk football rules are included in his work. We will however discount these. Let's look at the six ingredients of sport as they relate to rugby football:

LOCATION – Until 1845 the game was played on the Rugby School Close, but a set of rules was then printed, which allowed school leavers to take these with them and adapt the Football at Rugby rules to the location in which they were attempting to play the game. The 1862 rule book introduced a plan of the field, which allowed the Rugby School Rules to be played anywhere that had a large field. This standardised the 'location' and allowed rugby to be played anywhere in the world. The 1879 RFU laws were the first to introduce a pitch size:

"The Field of Play must not exceed 110 yards in length nor 75 yards in breadth..." – APRL001

PERSONNEL – The game was initially played by the boys of Rugby School and, in the earliest recollections of former players, any number of players was allowed; the teams were limited only by the house numbers and those who were unable to play. The first international in 1871 saw 20 players on each side. In 1875 the universities played 15 a-side and this became standard practice in 1876, but did not appear in the law books until 1892:

"It was not until 1892 that a law appeared in the Handbook which read: "The game should be played by 15 players on each side."" – APRL060

EQUIPMENT – It is thought that a rugby ball was initially a pig's bladder cased in leather. Its size and shape for Rugby Union became standardised in 1892:

"The game shall be played with an oval ball of as nearly as possible the following dimensions: length 11 inches to 11 ¼ inches; length in circumference 30 inches to 31 inches; width in circumference 25 ½ inches to 26 inches; weight 12 ounces to 13 ounces; hand sewn and not less than 8 stitches to the inch." – APRL027

ACTIONS – From the earliest set of rules we can deduce that there was a lot of kicking (punting, drop kicking & place kicks) and some catching and running involved and that hacking was allowed. It seems that knocking the ball on was allowable if a player made a fair catch when they were offside. In 2016, the object of the game is defined as:

"...two teams, each of fifteen players, observing fair play, according to the Laws and in a sporting spirit should, by carrying, passing, kicking and grounding the ball, score as many points as possible." – World Rugby website

This sets the modern day actions as being 'carrying, passing, kicking and grounding the ball'. Personally I'd add grappling or pushing for scrum time, jumping (line-out) and tackling to this list.

AIMS – The only aim during the developmental stages of Rugby Union – Football at Rugby School (until 1845) and Rugby School Rules (1845–1871) – was to score more goals than the opposition. This was the only known method of winning a game. This can also be said for the early period of Rugby Union itself, from 1871 to 1874. Up until that date it was impossible to win a game by scoring what we today call a 'try'. The term 'try' comes from a 'try at goal', which is what you were allowed to do after touching the ball down in your opponent's 'in goal' area. You were allowed a try at goal, i.e. a kick, and after 1875 it was this attempt at goal, if the kick was missed, that would win you the game if the goals were equal. In 1886, for the countries playing under International Board rules a points system was introduced such that the aim of the game became to score the most points:

"1886. It was again proposed to score by points, the object being to find out the better side, not the one with the best place kick: this was now adopted and the Law read: 'A match shall be decided by points: a goal shall equal 3 points and a try 1 point: if the number of points is equal or no goal be kicked or try obtained, the match shall be drawn: when a goal is kicked from a try, only the goal is scored." – APRL0031

The latter statement "*when a goal is kicked from a try, only the goal is scored*" remained in the rules up until 1979, highlighting the greater importance of the goal compared to the try. This was 156 years after the Webb Ellis event, so even though the overall aim of the game changed from goals to points, the easiest and most common way of obtaining those points, particularly in the early days of Rugby Union, was by scoring goals. It must be considered, therefore, that scoring goals was the main aim of the game up until the late 1970s. Even today the goal plays a huge part in the modern game, despite the number of points gained from scoring a try having increased to five. This is why when scoring a try players run behind the posts when they are able to. There can be no argument against the fact that for the majority of its existence, Rugby Union has been a kicking game.

At this point you may be shaking your head, believing that rugby is traditionally a running game. Let's look into this a bit further. Cast your mind back to the recent 2015 Rugby World Cup final. To win the William Webb Ellis Cup, New Zealand scored 34 points, with 15 points scored from tries and 19 points from goals. Let's look at the history of Rugby World Cup finals and the points scored from running *vs.* kicking the ball:

Year of RWC final	Points from tries	Points from goals
2015	25	26
2011	10	5
2007	0	21
2003	10	27
1999	10	37
1995	0	27
1991	4	14
1987	16	22
Totals	75	179

The evidence is conclusive. It's also important to note that in two of the above finals no tries were scored at all; incidentally both were won by South Africa. In only one of the above finals were more points scored from tries than from goals and ironically this was probably the dullest and least exciting of all the past finals, with the least amount of points scored too. Nowadays the game is more of a running one, but that is just the result of the natural evolution of the sport.

Scoring a goal remained the main aim of the game until the late 1970s, one hundred and fifty years after Webb Ellis is claimed to have invented a 'running game'. It is useful, however, to look at the evolution of the game so that we have a better understanding of how it changed from a predominantly kicking one to a running game.

We should look at information about the laws and how the game was played from the correspondence written by the former Rugby School pupils in the Old Rugbeian Society Report of 1897. The excerpts which follow are not in the order in which they were published in the report, but I have arranged them in chronological order instead as I believe that this will help us to understand the evolution of the game. We will however start with Matthew Bloxam's letter to the Meteor in 1880 that relates to his time at the school 1813–1820. Note that the aim of the report was to ascertain as to when running with the ball began at the school, so there will be much mention of running amongst the correspondence, but we should pay particular attention as to why the players were actually running. They were running to 'place try' at goal, which means that they would place the ball down in the open field of play and try a kick at goal. Kicking a goal was the only method of scoring both before and after the William Webb Ellis event.

1813–1820 – MATTHEW HOLBECHE BLOXAM – *"circa 1817–18, Bigside, both at cricket and football was removed to that part of the Close lying immediately south of the Headmaster's garden wall... The procedure at Bigside of Football was then as follows... When, then, all had assembled in the Close, two of the best players in the school commenced choosing in, one for each side. After choosing in about a score on each side, a somewhat rude division was made of the remaining fags, half of whom were sent to keep goal on the one side, the other half to the opposite goal for the same purpose. Any fag, though not specially chosen in might follow up on that side to the goal of which he was attached. Some of these were ready enough to mingle in the fray, others judiciously kept half back, watching their opportunity for a casual kick, which was not unfrequently awarded (sic) [afforded?] them. Few and simple were the rules of the game: touch on the sides of the ground was marked out, and no one was allowed to run with the ball in his grasp towards the opposite goal. It was Football, and not Handball, plenty of hacking but little struggling."* – ORSR008

1823-1825 – *"In the latter half of 1823... caught the ball in his arms. This being so, according to the then rule, he ought to have retired back as far as he pleased, without parting with the ball, for the combatants on the opposite side could only advance to the spot where he had caught the ball, and were unable to rush forward until he had either punted it or placed it for some one else to kick, for it was by means of these placed kicks that most of the goals were in those days kicked, but the moment the ball touched the ground, the opposite side might rush on... disregarded this rule, and on catching the ball, instead of retiring backwards, rushed forwards with the ball in his hands towards the opposite goal."* – ORSR009

1828 – THOMAS HARRIS – *"1. Picking up and running with the ball in hand was distinctly forbidden. If a player caught the ball on a rebound from the ground, or from the stroke of a hand, he was allowed to take a few steps so as to give effect to a 'Drop-kick,' but no more: subject of course to interruption from the adverse players... 2. If the ball was caught in the hands from a kick, the catcher was entitled to 'place try' at goal, retiring a sufficient distance from the place where the catch was made. 3. All laying hands upon and holding a player was strictly forbidden under any circumstances."* – ORSR020

1830 – JOHN COKE FOWLER – *"... my recollection of a great many games at Rugby is quite in accord with yours. Many a time I have caught and run with the ball in the way you describe, and rushed towards the goal to try a drop kick. But one was usually intercepted and obliged to put the ball down, before one's kick could send it over the bar. I have, however no knowledge of the practice before 1830..."* – ORSR024

1830–33 – H.G. ALLEN – *"I was playing that game pretty constantly from about 1830 to 1833, but as to carrying the ball, though I remember it was an occasional practice to do so, I cannot recall that there was any law on the subject. My impression is that it used to be carried until an opponent came so near as to be within what might be called kicking distance, say two or three feet, when it had to be thrown down between the two. This was the practice I am pretty sure..."* – ORSR023

1830–1834 – JOHN R. LYON – *"... I am satisfied that it was allowable to pick up the ball if you could, and run with it through the adversary's lines – dodging the players as well you could, and keeping your legs if possible in spite of hacks and collaring, and kicking a goal or touching the ball behind the post, to secure a try at goal."* – ORSR015

1830–1839 – FRANCIS HUGH DEANE – *"I believe that running with the ball in the arms, taken on the bound, prevailed in my time; but as a rule a mark was made from fair catches, and the player making the mark retired towards his own goal and took a drop or a punt. A successful drop could score a goal, but a punt could not. If the player made his mark within a reasonable distance of the goal posts, the ball was placed and a try attempted.*
I feel sure when a ball was thrown out of touch at right angles, that a player to whom it came might knock it on in the direction of the goal he was making for." – ORSR027

1830–40 – H.R. NEVILL (CANON NEVILL OF NORWICH) – *"If the ball were fairly caught before touching the ground, it was lawful to run as far as possible, and any kick, punt or drop kick was allowed.*
If the ball had touched the ground and was then caught on the bound, it was lawful to run, but only a drop kick was allowed.
If the ball were thrown by hand especially from the trees, the ball must be thrown down, no punt or drop, or running was counted fair.
If however it were kicked out from "touch," it was treated as in other cases; if caught in the air or on the first bound, running if possible was allowed.
But in no case and under no circumstances was it fair to take up the ball from the ground and run: whether still or rolling it might only be kicked as it was found." – ORSR026

1831– R.W. PEREGRINE BIRCH (son of) – *"... the ball could not be "picked up," but that, if caught, it could be carried as long as, physically speaking, the carrier was allowed to do so. I tried to learn whether the ball had to be caught before it touched the ground, or whether it might have been caught on first bounce; and I fancy from what he said the first bounce would have done..."* – ORSR025

1831 – SAMUEL GARRETT – *"The practice of running with the ball and being hacked down by the pursuers was in vogue when I entered the School."* – ORSR025

1832 – ALEX J. ARBUTHNOT – *"When I went to Rugby in 1832 the practice of running with the ball was in full force..."* – ORSR019

1832–36 – H.H. GIBBS (Lord Aldenham) – *"I can hardly think that the practice of running with the ball was "only gradually coming into vogue" in his day. I well remember that it was fully recognised in mine which ended in 1836. At what time it began in those four years, if it did not begin before, I can't say, but I certainly remember no time when it was considered absolutely illegitimate. But anyone who practised it set in more active motion the legs of his opponents for the purposes both of running and "hacking"... Probably from what you quote from Bloxam it must have arisen between 1820 and 1830 and very likely in the year to which he assigns it."* – ORSR014

1834 – THOMAS HUGHES – *"In my first year, 1834, running with the ball to get a try by touching down within goal was not absolutely forbidden, but a jury of Rugby boys of that day would almost certainly have found a verdict of "justifiable homicide" if a boy had been killed in running in. The practice grew, and was tolerated more and more, and indeed became rather popular in 1838–39 from the prowess of Jem Mackie the great 'runner in.'"* – ORSR012

1835 – GEORGE CHAS. BENN – *"I do not remember any rules against running with the ball, but picking it up from the ground was considered decidedly wrong and not allowed. If the ball was caught on the first bound, it was quite legitimate, when there seemed to be a chance of getting through, to run with it, and, if no chance presented itself, a drop kick was the usual custom... Running with the ball was certainly in existence in my time, but I do not remember any sort of plan of passing it from one to the other that time."* – ORSR018

1838–39 – F. LUSHINGTON – *"It was done in my time, that is in the autumns of 1838–39, when I was coming to the front in football, but I should say not done very often. I remember trying it on myself on one occasion in particular, when I got particularly neatly hacked over for my pains. But it certainly was never objected to, as far as I remember, and therefore must have been recognised as a regular part of the game, as we were extremely strict about all off-side rules then."* – ORSR016

1841–42 – THOMAS HUGHES – *"... I was captain of 'Big Side' in 1841–42 when we settled it (as we believed) for all time. 'Running in' was made lawful with these limitations, (1) that the ball must be caught on the bound, that the catcher was not "off his side" that there should be no "handing on," but the catcher must carry the ball in and "touch down" himself. Picking up off the ground was made absolutely illegal, as were running in from off your side – a ball caught by a player "off his side" must be at once knocked on or the holder might be mauled; and no handing on was allowed."* – ORSR012

The first set of rules drawn up in 1845 includes 'running in' – touching the ball between the goal posts – and 'try at goal' – attempting to kick a goal after the ball has been run in. This involved two kicks: a punt from the try line to the kicker and then a place kick from infield.

"... and it must go over the bar and between the posts without having touched the dress or person of any player." – FORU008

"Rule xxxiv. At little sides the goals shall be four paces wide, and in kicking a goal the ball must pass out of the reach of any player present." – FORU016

Little sides was the next area over from Bigside, where the main games were played. Rule xxxiv shows that kicking goals was part of the game. As this first set of rules was drawn up for games that were only to be played at Rugby School, no aim or object of the game was included – the lawmakers (of which there were three) presumed that every participant knew that the object of the game was to score a goal.

"Rule xx. All matches are drawn after five days, but after three if no goal has been kicked." – FORU013

This rule proves that the only object of the game was to score a goal and that no other method of winning existed. 'Running in' only allowed you a 'try' at kicking a goal and running with the ball had no bearing on the result of a game, apart from if a goal was scored as a result of this action. Running with the ball was thus not an aim of the game, but just another action within the play.

In the introduction to the 1862 set of Rugby School Rules it states:

"The object of the game is to kick the ball over the adversary's goal, which can be done either by dropping a goal or placing a goal: the former in the course of the game..." – JMRB096

If we refer back to Bloxam's Meteor Article and the nature of the game in 1813–1820:

"...for it was by means of these placed kicks that most of the goals were in those days kicked..." – ORSR010

As no change in the object of the game is mentioned by any of the pupils in the above extracts, or by Bloxam in his writings, the object of the game in Bloxam's time must have been to score as many goals as possible to win the game, otherwise such a change of objective would have been recorded. In 'Tom Brown's Schooldays' (1857), written by the previously quoted Thomas Hughes, the game, which was set in the 1830s, was played to the best of three goals, with the first to two goals winning the game. Following on from the 1862 Rugby School Rules, we can see that the goal has been the main objective of the game for the majority of the sport's existence:

1874 – The Rugby Football Union state:

"A match shall be decided by a majority of goals only." – APRL031

1875 – This was changed to:

"A match shall be decided by a majority of goals, but if the number of goals is equal or no goal be kicked, by a majority of tries." – APRL031

'Tries' in this case referred to when a kick at goal was attempted and missed after the ball had been placed behind the posts. Placing the ball down behind the line, what we now know as the 'try', was at that time known as the 'touch down'. It was the missed kick, the 'try at goal', that scored the point, not the 'touch down'.

1877 – "*When a goal is kicked from a try only the goal is scored.*" – APRL031

1883 – The game was still dominated by kicking. The first three rules in the 1883 laws explain the types of kicks that were allowed – drop kick, place kick & punt – and provide their definitions, and the next two rules relate to the goal, the size of the posts and how to score a goal. The rules of the game relating to what we now know as the 'try' are extremely complicated. In 1883 this feat was called the 'run in' and it had no value. When a player crossed the line with the ball they put it down and then had the choice to bring the ball out from the goal line where they had touched it down and place it for another of their side to kick the ball and have a 'try at goal', or they could 'punt out' from the goal line. In the latter case, if the 'punt out' was caught by a player of their own side in the field of play, the player could either make a fair catch and have a 'try at goal' through a drop kick or place kick or they could 'punt on' to restart the game. The 'punt on' would then allow their team to attempt another 'touch down'. We must assume that a player would attempt the 'punt out' if they scored the 'touch down' near to the corner of the field in too awkward a position for a 'try at goal'. The following rules in the 1883 laws relate to this system:

"7 – A match shall be decided by a majority of goals; but if the number of goals be equal, or no goal be kicked, by a majority of tries. If no goal be kicked or try obtained,

the match shall be drawn. Where a goal is kicked from a try, the goal only is scored." – CAFA017

"15 – *It is lawful for any player who has the ball to run with it and if he does so, it is called a RUN. If a player runs with the ball until he gets behind his opponents' goal line, and there touches it down, it is called a RUN IN*". – CAFA018

"9 – A TOUCH DOWN is when a player, putting his hand upon the ball on the ground in touch or in goal, stops it so that it remains dead, or fairly so." – CAFA018

"6 – A TRY is gained when a player touches the ball down in his opponents' in goal." – CAFA017

"47 – If a TRY AT GOAL be made by a place kick, a player of the side which has touched the ball down shall bring it up to the goal line (subject to Rule 48), in a straight line from the goal line opposite to the spot where the ball was touched down, and there make a mark on the goal line, and thence walk straight out with it at right angles to the goal line, such distance as he thinks proper, and there place it for another of his side to kick. The kicker's side must be behind the ball when it is kicked, and the opposite side must remain behind the goal line until the ball has been placed on the ground. (See Rules 54 and 55)." – CAFA021

"48 – If the ball has been touched down between the goal posts, it must be brought out in a straight line from either of such posts." – CAFA021

"29 – A PUNT OUT is a punt made after a touch down, by a player from behind his opponents' goal-line towards his own side, who must stand outside the goal line and endeavour to make a fair catch or to get the ball and run in or drop a goal." – CAFA020

"30 – A PUNT ON is a punt made in a manner similar to a punt out, and from touch, if necessary, by a player who has made a fair catch from a punt out or another punt on." – CAFA020

The above rules tell us that the 'run in', the modern day try, had no value in 1883; the aim was still to score as many goals as possible. If you took the punt out option after a 'run in', it was the punt itself that scored the point. If, however, you scored in the corner and there was a howling gale in your face and your 'try at goal' kick failed to lift off the floor, as long as you kicked the ball, that is, you had a 'try at goal', this missed kick would have won you the match had the goals scored been even at the end of the game. At this point 60 years had passed since the Webb Ellis event and even though running was part of the game and passing had also been introduced, the aim of the game was still to kick the ball between the posts and over the crossbar. After this point we do however start to see a change, where a try (at goal) was scored after the touch down, no matter what type of kick was made.

1886 – For the first time a side could lose a game despite having scored more goals than the opposition; although this would have been a very rare occurrence:

"It was again proposed to score by points, the object being to find out the better side, not the one with the best place kick: this was now adopted and the Law read: 'A match shall be decided by points: a goal shall equal 3 points and a try 1 point: if the number of points is equal or no goal be kicked or try obtained, the match shall be drawn: when a goal is kicked from a try, only the goal is scored." – APRL0031

1887 – An example of this points system in action – in the international at Birkenhead Park between Wales and Ireland, the Welsh team ran out winners after a dropped goal and a try (3 + 1 = 4 points) against Ireland's three tries (3 x 1 = 3 points).

1889 – The Rugby Football Union, who had refused to join the International Board, were playing with the following scoring method:

"A match shall be decided by a majority of points: a goal shall equal 3 points, with the exception of a goal kicked from a kick awarded by way of a penalty, which shall equal 2 points, and a try one point; If the number of points is equal or no goal be kicked or try obtained the match shall be drawn; when a goal is kicked from a try, the goal only is scored." – APRL032

The International Board on the other hand were playing with this scoring system:

"A match shall be decided by a majority of points: a goal from a try shall equal 4 points, a dropped goal or one from a fair catch 3 points, and a try 2 points. If the number of points is equal or no goal be kicked or try obtained, the match shall be drawn. When a goal is kicked from a try, only the goal is scored." – APRL032

1905 – In their last game in Britain before moving on to France, the All Blacks played Swansea and won by a dropped goal, scoring four points to a try worth three points by the Welsh club. The dropped goal was worth more than the try until 1948 and was then of equal value until the early 1970s.

1948 – The dropped goal was reduced to three points and a penalty goal was also worth three points, as was a try, but if a goal worth five points was scored after the try, then the try itself didn't score.

1978 – In the year that Wales won its eighth Grand Slam title under the captaincy of Phil Bennett, a try still didn't count if the goal after it was successful. Below are excerpts from the Laws of the Game of Rugby Football, as framed by the International Rugby Football Board for that year:

"The Object of the Game is that two teams of 15 players each, observing fair play according to the Laws and a sporting spirit, should by carrying, passing and kicking the ball score as many points as possible, the team scoring the greater number of points to be the winner of the match." – WRUH002

"Law 11 Method of Scoring

Try. A try is scored by first grounding the ball in the opponent's In-goal.

Goal. A goal is scored by kicking the ball over the opponents' crossbar and between the goal posts from the field-of-play by any place kick or drop kick.

The scoring values are as follows...

A try	*4 points*
A goal from a try (in which case the try shall not count)	*6 points*
A goal from a penalty kick	*3 points*
A dropped goal otherwise attained	*3 points"* – WRUH014

Even in 1978 the goal had the highest points value and when scored it erased the value of the try. To score a goal was therefore still a team's main aim during a game of Rugby Union.

The laws were changed the following year, in 1979, when the value of the goal from a try was reduced to 2 points and the clause 'in which case the try shall not count' was dropped.

2015 – New Zealand won the Rugby World Cup by scoring 34 points to Australia's 17. 19 of those points come from goals and only 15 from tries. Even in 2015, the goal was still king.

RULES – Matthew Bloxam's accounts of Football at Rugby School during his time there 1813–1820 prove that there was a verbal set of rules in place at the school. The game he describes is well organized and well established and is the same game that Webb Ellis was playing in 1823. The Bigside Levée, a group of senior pupils, was in charge of the verbal rules before the first rules were laid down in 1845. This same set of rules evolved from 1845 through to the 2016 rules laid down by today's Rugby Union governing body, World Rugby.

THE INGREDIENTS WITH RESPECT TO THE ORIGIN

Let's look at the above 6 ingredients of Rugby Union with respect to the previously held theories of its origin – that folk football is the parent game or that the Webb Ellis event can be considered the birth of rugby football.

1) Webb Ellis

In the progression of a sport, as outlined previously, the difference between step 5 (play) and step 6 (game) is the absence or presence of verbal rules. Whilst step 5 does have an aim to the play, there is neither an outcome nor a contest. With the addition of rules, either verbal or written, there is a structure to the play and the aim is governed by the rules so that an outcome is assured. Matthew Bloxam's description of the game in his day stated that Football at Rugby School already had rules before Webb Ellis and that Webb Ellis had broken a rule. So Football at Rugby School was already a game. For Webb Ellis to have then invented a different game, this game would have had to have been 'created' and he would have had to have significantly altered some of the six key ingredients and taken his new game forward, away from the recognized game which was already in –existence – Football at Rugby School. This was not the case. The game existed before Webb Ellis and the same game was played in the same location, with the same personnel, with the same equipment, using the same actions, aims and rules after he broke those rules. When Webb Ellis left the school in 1825, there is no record that anything in the game had changed from when he had entered it seven years earlier. In brief:

	Before WWE event	After WWE event	Result
Location	Rugby School	Rugby School	No change
Personnel	Pupils at Rugby School	Pupils at Rugby School	No change
Equipment	Ball	Ball	No change
Action	Kick & hit ball forward	Kick & hit ball forward	No change
Aim	To score a goal	To score a goal	No change
Rules	Verbal as agreed by the players	Verbal as agreed by the players	No change

If we compare this to the 'creation' of Rugby League in 1895, we can see how this led to changes in some of the ingredients:

	Before	After	Result
Location	Rugby pitch	Rugby pitch	No change
Personnel	All Rugby Union players in England	Northern Union teams only	Change
Equipment	Ball	Ball	No change

Action	Carry, pass & kick ball	Carry, pass & kick ball	No change
Aim	To win the game by scoring more points than the other team	To win the game by scoring more points than the other team	No change
Rules	As laid down by the International Board, including retaining an amateur status.	Northern Union Rules, the 'Broken time' payment rule is added.	Change

In that case there were two changes within the six ingredients, neither of which changed the actual game being played. The main thing that changed was the personnel. Because the thirty Yorkshire and Lancashire clubs formed the Northern Union, which became a breakaway governing body, a new sport was created. They were playing the same game as the Rugby Football Union were, but because they were now a separate unit, they moved onto a different evolutionary path. The breakaway enabled them to adapt their game, setting it apart from the one that the Rugby Football Union played. That is why Rugby League and Rugby Union are today similar, yet different.

2) Folk football

It is possible that a game of folk football arrived at Rugby School with a headmaster or some pupils and was a parent or contributory game to Football at Rugby School, but I believe this possibility to be extremely slight. Considering the number of differences between Football at Rugby School and the folk football games recorded by Shearman & Marshall, it is highly unlikely. Consider our ingredients list and in particular the aims. The aim of folk football in the majority of cases was to carry a ball and touch it against something or take it through the posts, while the aim of Football at Rugby School from its earliest recording was to kick a ball between the posts and over the crossbar. Different aims in different locations add up to different games. Had folk football survived at Rugby School, surely some pupils would have recorded their experiences of it and some record would exist. Shearman & Marshall's records cannot be counted because they cannot provide evidence of any links between folk football and Football at Rugby School. To err on the safe side let's look at the various elements involved. In this case we are looking at rugby being an evolution of folk football, so we are now looking for evidence of similarities, as opposed to a change in an element as for the alleged Webb Ellis creation event.

	Football at Rugby School	Folk football	Similarities
Location	Rugby School	Lots of places, but no evidence for it at Rugby School	No evidence

Personnel	Pupils at Rugby School	Players at the various locations, but no evidence of it having been played by pupils at Rugby School	No evidence
Equipment	Ball	Ball of some description	Similar
Action	Kick & hit ball forward	Mostly carrying ball to opposition's goal	No evidence
Aim	To score a goal by kicking the ball between the uprights over a crossbar	To move a ball through two posts or other objects	No evidence
Verbal rules	Football at Rugby School verbal rules	Folk Football verbal rules	Written records indicate different rules, with one rule (kick off in the middle) being the same

The only similarities between the recorded forms of folk football and Football at Rugby School are the ball and the kick off being performed in the middle of the area of play. There is no evidence of a link between any form of folk football and Football at Rugby School, but without a definite conclusive 'origin theory' for Rugby Union, we cannot rule out the possibility that Rugby Union is descended from folk football.

SUMMARY – Now that we have concluded our analysis of Rugby Union we can move on to decide on a point of origin. We've identified that the aim of scoring a goal by kicking a ball over the crossbar and between the posts has to be considered as having been the most important factor in Rugby Union over its entire existence. In the early developmental stages of Rugby Union this was the only means by which a game could be won. When the overall objective aim of the game changed to the winning team being the one that scored the most points, the goal after securing a 'try at goal', and in more recent years a goal after scoring a try, was still the method of securing the highest number of points available. In 1979, the scoring method changed so that a 'running' score became the highest individual value, and even so a high percentage of games are today won from kicking rather than running scores. Webb Ellis played a kicking game with actions, aims and rules that, according to Matthew Bloxam, did not change while he was at the school. Therefore, the origin of Rugby Union must pre-date the William Webb Ellis event.

Scoring a goal by kicking a ball over the crossbar and between the posts is also what has set Rugby Union apart from all forms of folk football, all other school games and later Association football.

CONCLUSION – From the above analysis we can conclude that the moment that Rugby Union became recognizable as an individual entity was when the aim of the game during its developmental stage of Football at Rugby School became to score a goal by kicking the ball over the crossbar and between the posts. This aim must pre-date Matthew Bloxam's arrival at the school in 1813.

FOOTNOTE – I think that we're getting somewhere now. I can see a speck of light at the end of the tunnel. Further analysis of Football at Rugby School is needed to decide how and at what point the goal became the origin. Altogether, straight into the chorus to the tune of Queen's 'We will rock you'.........

We will, we will kick you
We will, we will kick you
The origin of rugby it lies with the goal
Above the bar and between the poles
We will, we will kick you
We will, we will kick you

CHAPTER 8 – WAS FOOTBALL AT RUGBY SCHOOL CREATED?

AIM – To analyse whether or not Football at Rugby School was created there.

It is widely accepted that Rugby Union is descended from Football at Rugby School, with the earliest accepted point of origin being the William Webb Ellis event. Therefore, we need to look at the origin of Football at Rugby School to decide as to whether this is also the origin of Rugby Union.

The earliest accepted record of Football at Rugby School is in the book 'Macready's Reminiscences and Selections from his Diaries and Letters', edited by Sir Frederick Pollock Bart and published in 1875.

William Charles Macready

William Charles Macready went on to be a famous actor after attending Rugby School 1803–1808. The first chapter of the book deals with his early reminiscences, including the years he spent at Rugby School. In the passage in which he mentions football, Macready was called away from playing the game in the school close by the headmaster Dr Ingles. As Dr Ingles left Rugby School in 1806, to be replaced by Dr Wooll, this meeting must have taken place sometime between 1803 and 1806.

"I recollect one day, when playing foot-ball in the school close, Dr Inglis was walking on the gravel walk that surrounds it." – MRFP011

Ingles (spelt incorrectly as Inglis by Macready) then interviewed Macready as to his career intentions. Macready could see his future in law and the headmaster questioned him as to whether or not he had considered his father's profession. Macready senior was a theatre manager and part-time actor but Macready was insistent that he wished to go to the Bar and become a barrister. Happy with this choice, Ingles refrained from giving the advice he sought to impart and the conversation ended. Unfortunately, Macready's father would go on to make a poor investment in a Manchester theatre and young William would feel honour-bound to abandon his aspirations and would go on to pursue an acting career in order to help with the family finances.

There are two potential options for the creation of Football at Rugby School that I can see. The first is that a group of boys and/or masters sat down together and drew up a set of plans for the game, and the second is that Football at Rugby has a parent game that was introduced to the school and that Football at Rugby School is a descendant of this game. We have already explored the possibility that ancient folk football is the parent or ancestor game for rugby and we found that to be highly unlikely.

THE ETON LINK

There is, however, one School game that raises its hand and claims that it could be the predecessor of Football at Rugby School. That game is Football at Eton School. I am not the first to identify this possibility; in their 1969 Oxford University history, Ross McWhirter & Sir Andrew Noble offered this opinion:

"Once given a field it would be almost unnatural if schoolboys did not play. Rugby at that time had two successive headmasters from Eton who therefore knew all about the Field Game: Rev Dr. Thomas James, D.D. (1778 to 1794) and then Dr. Henry Ingles, D.D. (1794 to 1806)." – RMOU012

RUGBY'S ETON-EDUCATED HEADMASTERS

Let's look at the headships of these two masters through the words of HC Bradby B.A. in his book 'Rugby' in the 'Handbook to the Great Public Schools' series (1900 Bell & Sons, London). This is what he says about James:

"... one of the most distinguished of Rugby head masters, and the first to bear that title, Thomas James, an Etonian and fellow of King's, commonly spoken of in Rugby at the present day as James the First." – HCBR035

Rev Dr Thomas James

"Under him, the school took its position as one of the leading English public schools, and the numbers increased rapidly: the year after he came there were only eighty boys; eleven years later, in 1790, there were 240... His mental abilities were of no mean order, but his success was due not so much to his capacities as a scholar and a mathematician, but to his abundant energy, which displayed itself in the organization of the school down to the minutest details: in this organization he had little foundation to work on, for none of his predecessors had been called upon to govern anything like such a large number of boys, and it says much for the merit of his work that, through the manifold changes that have been made during the last century, much of it remains intact. The system which he introduced was based on the Eton system, under which he had been educated. The school was divided into six forms; the Sixth was the highest, and (like the Fifth) has survived as a name, though the reason for it has passed away. The routine of work for all forms was most carefully arranged. It consisted mainly of translation from Latin and Greek authors, and composition in these languages, but it was not exclusively classical: Bible History alternating with the Histories of Rome and England, modern geography and Milton all find a place in the regular curriculum of the Sixth and Fifth, while modern languages and mathematics, which latter study James himself greatly loved, although they were "extras," were encouraged.

James's arrangement of school hours has in the main survived, the principle being that on whole school days there should be five lessons, one before breakfast, prepared overnight, two before dinner, and two more in the afternoon, and it is from this period that the three half-holidays on Tuesday, Thursday and Saturday are inherited, though at this time the Thursday half holiday was not a regular one, but only given in honour of specially good work done by some member of the Sixth, "play for So-and-So" being the formula under which the good news was announced. The forms were very large, six masters being considered a reasonable number for a school of 200 boys, and James introduced the Eton tutorial system... and it is a further testimony to the character of the head master that he was able on these terms to attract such men as the two Sleaths, afterwards head masters respectively of Repton and St Paul's, Innes, head master of Warwick School, Philip Homer, renowned as a Greek scholar, and Richard Bloxam, himself, an old Rugbeian, and father of the well-known antiquary." (Matthew Bloxam) – HCBR035

In this quite extensive account of James' period as headmaster, the author continues with his account of the memories of an old pupil from James' reign:

""A sort of saturnalia," writes an old pupil in his reminiscences, "followed the speeches" (they were then held in June, at the end of the half year).The last few days of the half year were spent in all kinds of riotous excesses. No lessons were expected to be done, excepting after a manner chosen by the boys – that is to say, anyhow; and half the windows of the school were broken, to be paid for by the parents, for the benefit of the Rugby glaziers" – HCBR042

In the same book, Henry Ingles' praises were not so well sung:

"James was succeeded by another Etonian and Fellow of King's, Henry Ingles, who well sustained the credit of the school during his twelve years of mastership. The numbers indeed fell by about fifty, but numbers are not always a sure indication of the efficiency of a school. He was a gloomy man, saddened by a terrible shock he had received when he had suddenly and unexpectedly met men carrying home the body of his eldest son, who had been accidentally drowned: it is related of him that, when one of the masters told him of the victory of Trafalgar, and added, "but I am sorry to say, sir, Lord Nelson is dead," he replied, "And I wish I were dead also." He made few changes in the school..." – HCBR044

The dialogue continues, mostly with the Great Rebellion of 1797 that occurred during Ingles' headship. It is noteworthy that he is reported to have made few changes in the school, as opposed to Thomas James who was said to have introduced a new system to the school – that based on the Eton system.

THOMAS JAMES AT RUGBY SCHOOL

Let's return to the end of the reminiscences of the former pupil, where *"saturnalia"* is mentioned. I had to get my Oxpop out to see what this means and I've learnt that saturnalia is the ancient Roman festival of Saturn, observed as a time of unrestrained merry making. After a little research I discovered that the primary source for this quote is former pupil Charles Apperley, also known as 'Nimrod', which was the pen name he used while writing for 'The Sporting Magazine'.

Charles Apperley "Nimrod"

The quote can be found in the book 'My Life and Times', authored by Nimrod (Charles Apperley) and edited by E.D Cuming, which is a compilation of Nimrod's autobiographical writings. Apperley's memories initially appeared as articles in ten installments of Fraser's Magazine – the first in January 1842. He entered Rugby School in 1789, eleven years into the Rev Dr Thomas James' headship. In the book, his memories of Rugby School stretch to two chapters and leafing forward a few pages from the 'saturnalia' quote we find the following passage:

Rugby school, in my time, sent forth some clever men into the literary world... Walter Savage Landor...He had a great name in the school as a scholar, a cricketer, a football player, and a pugilist, in all which characters he had very few equals... James was proud of Landor, and was inclined to cultivate his friendship as well as his mind; but, to use a common expression, Landor would not have him at any price..." – CALT144

Walter Savage Landor

Apperley states that Landor had a great name in the school as a scholar, cricketer, footballer and pugilist. In the book he goes into much greater detail about his school work, cricket and pugilism, but fails to mention football again. As Landor is said to have been a 'football player' at the school, it must be agreed by all that football was played at Rugby School by Walter Savage Landor who entered the school in 1783 and left circa 1791/1792 (RSRE1783). If football was invented at the school during Landor's time there, it would have been recorded by Apperley who roomed for four years with Samuel Butler, a contemporary of Landor. Therefore we must accept that the game Football at Rugby School was being played in the school when Landor started there in 1783. This is now the earliest date at which we can accept that football was played at Rugby School.

Landor pre-dated headmaster Henry Ingles, so if Football at Rugby School was created from Football at Eton, only Etonian Thomas James could have possibly introduced it to Rugby School. In his 1898 history of Rugby School, WH Rouse says of the Eton system that James introduced:

"James brought with him to Rugby Cambridge scholarship and Eton methods. We shall soon find not merely the tutorial system in full swing, and a body of præpostors served by fags, but dames' houses, and other things and customs which speak of the same origin. Even the very books used at Eton were to be transplanted to Rugby. In this

remodelling James was assisted by another Etonian, James Chartes, also fellow of King's whom the Trustees at the same time appointed to be Second Master." – WRRS129

The key words in the above quote are *"and other things and customs which speak of the same origin."* I think it safe to say that one of those other things and customs could have been Eton Football.

Did the boys of Rugby School have the opportunity to play football? They had the space – the Close was large although there were fences between the fields. They had the time – the new system included three half-day holidays in a six-day week: Tuesday, Thursday and Saturday, although the Thursday half-day at that time was only granted as a reward for good school work. James had a system whereby he would announce towards the end of the Thursday third lesson the pupils who were worthy of the half day holiday. Rouse states:

"Then if after third lesson the welcome sound was heard of "Play for Butler" or "Play for Landor," the boys would hasten over their work in anticipation of a fine afternoon's sport." – WRRS159

Charles Apperley spent four years rooming with Samuel Butler, who was to become Bishop of Lichfield and headmaster of Shrewsbury School, but he could not understand how Butler regularly won the opportunity of play from James:

"How then did he acquire the reputation of being the best scholar in the school; and how was it that "Play for Butler" (i.e., a whole holiday for the best exercise of the week) was oftener proclaimed for him than any other boy?" – CALT142

I think it fair to say from the above that James encouraged the leisure activities of the boys at the school. He was in close contact with the boys he taught in both the fifth and sixth forms (WRRS137), so he was face to face for most of the day with the 'leaders' of the school. Conversations about James' time at Eton and what they did at Eton for play most probably took place. Not forgetting of course that the assistant master James Chartes was also ex-Eton, so he too could have been singing the praises of the 'old Eton game'. If Football at Eton pre-dates Football at Rugby School, then it is possible that Football at Eton is the parent game of Football at Rugby School.

HISTORY OF FOOTBALL AT ETON

It is possible that football was played at Eton as early as in the late 1400s. A former headmaster of Eton, William Horman (c1440–1535), wrote the following in his Latin textbook 'The Vulgaria' published in 1519:

"Lusui erit nobis follies pugilari spirtu tumens"

"We will play with a ball full of wynde."

Horman was headmaster at Eton between 1485 and 1494. From there he went to Winchester (1495–1501), another school with an important football history, and then returned to Eton as a fellow and vice-provost until his death in 1535. Although the book was published in 1519, he says in the introduction that he composed the book as a schoolmaster "*many years before*" (LCFG014).

In Chapter 27, 'Of the Ball', in his 1581 book 'Positions Wherein Those Primitive Circumstances Be Examined, Which Are Necessarie for the Training up of Children', Richard Mulcaster mentions three types of ball games – hand ball, footeball and armeball. He describes footeball as being an unruly dangerous sport and not a healthy pastime:

"...with thronging of a rude multitude, with bursting of shinnes, and breaking of legges, it be neither ciuil, neither worthy the name of any traine to health." – RMPW105

It is commonly accepted amongst modern historians that Mulcaster's mentioning of a training maister (coach), judge (referee) and smaller teams implies that these were in use at the time, but looking at the below extract I would say that this is a point of contention and that Mulcaster has merely taken these terms from military terminology. Rather than stating that these were already a part of the game, I would argue that he was a visionary who suggested that 'any man' could see that these three improvements would alter the game of football and that they would benefit the health of children should they play the game. The passage below was written in the 16th century so the English is not as we know it. In most cases the letters 'u' and 'v' are transposed compared to what we are now used to.

"Wherin any man may euidently see the use of the trayning maister. For if one stand by, which can judge of the play, and is judge over the parties, and hath authoritie to commaunde in the place, all those inconueniences haue bene, I know, and wilbe I am sure very lightly redressed, nay they will neuer entermedle in the matter, neither shall there be complaint, where there is no cause. Some smaller number with such ouerlooking, sorted into sides and standings, not meeting with their bodies so boisterously to trie their strength: nor shouldring or shuffing one an other so barbarously, and vsing to walke after, may vse footeball for as much good to the body, by the chiefe vse of the legges..." – RMPW106

Mulcaster was a big fan of Girolamo Mecuriale, the Italian physician who wrote 'De Arte Gymnastica', which is considered to be the first book on sports medicine. At the time of writing he had been incumbent as the first headmaster of the Merchant Taylors' School in London but he was also an old Etonian.

Although there is no supporting evidence that can give us the date of the origin of football at Eton, it is recognized that Football at Eton pre-dates Football at Rugby School. In his recent 'Eton Field Game' Lachlan Campbell states that in the eighteenth century:

"Eton was playing a game called 'Goals', a primitive form of football, as well as a newer game (the Wall Game) played against the new wall along the Slough Road, built in 1717." – LCFG016

In his 1911 'A History of Eton College', Maxwell-Lyte attributes the earliest accepted origin of Football at Eton to around 1766 thanks to a manuscript prepared by Rev JCB Riddell, called Nugae Etonenses (MLEC316), which includes a list of games played at the school. The document has been dated by Eton historians based on the events that happened around that time at the college, so this date can be regarded as being fairly accurate. Within the list are games called 'Goals' & 'Scrambling Walls' (MLEC318), which are possibly the games that were later known as the Lower College game and the Wall Game. Football (MLEC319) is also mentioned, which Maxwell-Lyte states *"was almost certainly the game as played in the Field"* (the Field Game). These games will have been played in the 'football fields' (MLEC322), which are also mentioned in another part of the same manuscript. For there to have been football fields at Eton in 1766, it must be accepted that football was played there at around that time, and therefore Eton Football pre-dates Thomas James' headmastership at Rugby School by at least 12 years. The question that we should now ask is:

IS ETON FOOTBALL THE PARENT SPORT OF FOOTBALL AT RUGBY SCHOOL?

In the early 1800s, Eton School (now College) had three versions of football. Let's look at how these compare to Football at Rugby School:

THE WALL GAME – This game still exists today and is played against a wall that is 110 metres long. The wall was erected in 1717, so the game originated after that date. The game is more of a school cultural tradition than a contest. There is little movement as the game consists of a group of boys pressed against a wall trying to force a ball to move along it. I would go as far as to suggest that the game could also be described as dangerous boredom. There are few differing tactics and goals are extremely rare; in fact periods of over 100 years where no goals were scored at all exist in its history. There is no real comparison to Football at Rugby School.

THE LOWER COLLEGE GAME – This game ceased to exist after 1865, most likely because the ground on which it was played was sold or became unusable. In his 1917 book 'Memories of Eton Sixty Years Ago', Arthur Campbell Ainger provides the best description of how this game was played. In describing the various forms of football at Eton, he talks about the 'fields of play':

"It lay across the road to Sheep's bridge and on it was played a game called 'Lower College'. This was football reduced to its simplest elements. There were two goals marked on trees – the traces of one goal can yet be seen, the other tree has fallen long since. A "bully" was formed as usual, and one had either to kick the ball against the goal or to run it behind the line and touch it. It was not necessary to be "bullied" on the line in any way. For touching it one claimed a "shy" and was entitled to "boss" the ball at the goal, in front of which the opposing Eleven stood, so a goal was rarely obtained. The game was abandoned in 1865..." – AAME164

As the game ceased to be played in the 1860s and no other information for its methods of play exists, from the above account we can deduce that the goals were low and not high – once a 'shy' was scored, the conversion, called a 'boss', was taken with 11 players standing in front of the goal, and hardly any goals were scored. Unless the players were standing on each other's shoulders, the goals must have been low down rather than high up. The use of trees as goals is however interesting considering the number of trees in the Close at Rugby School.

THE FIELD GAME – Again from Ainger's book:

"In College Field the ordinary "Field" game was played, but in a much more rough-and-ready fashion than now. The goal-sticks had no crossbar; there were sticks at the four corners of the ground, but no lines were cut in the turf or otherwise marked either at the base or on the sides. Consequently the player very often did not know when he was near the line or over it – the umpire, when there was one, judged the point by looking along from the goal-post to the post at the corner and deciding as best he could. It followed that little or no attempt was made at the slow and elaborate progress along the line which is now in fashion – one went at once either for the goal or for a "rouge" off one of the opposite players – one failed probably much more often than not, but less time was wasted. It is our only object here to record matters, not to decide which system was best." – AAME164

Of the three versions, the Lower College game looks to be the most similar to Football at Rugby School, but few records of the game exist. The Eton Field game, or to give it its correct title 'Football as played in the field at Eton' was more widely recorded in history. Although it is recorded that the first written rules for any form of football were laid down at Eton in 1815, these have not survived and so we'll need to check out the oldest surviving sets of rules of football as played at Rugby and Eton. These are dated 1845 for Rugby School and 1847 for the Field Game at Eton. We will only compare the rules that relate to the nature of how the game was played, as several rules from both sets relate to discipline or timings and are quite lengthy. Firstly, however, let's clarify why we should do this.

RULES, REGULATIONS & LAWS

The rules or laws of a game can give clues as to, or tell us how, a game was played. They are the best source of information when it comes to the aims and actions of the players in the game. These two sets of rules are however the first written rules and there are therefore no previous sets of rules to compare them against, apart from the recollections of the players and their memories of the verbal rules. Neither set of rules mentions how many players there should be to a team, the size of the pitch, or even the shape, size and type of ball to be played with. These are all believed to be presumed knowledge by the law makers. What we are looking for in the two sets of laws are similarities. If we compare Rugby League to its parent sport, Rugby Union, we can find lots of similarities in the actions (running, passing, kicking, catching, scrummaging), aims (scoring goals and tries), and in the terminology (try, goal, scrummage, tackle *etc.*). Rugby League split from Rugby Union 120 years ago and the sports are still similar. If Thomas James did introduce Football at Eton to Rugby School then we are looking at a smaller timeframe, with just over 60 years from its introduction to the first written laws. We know that the main additions to Football at Rugby School in the 1830s were the introduction of the touch down and running forward with the ball, so if we ignore these two features then we will have a better idea of how the game was played at Rugby School around the turn of the 19th century, so as to compare it with the Field Game at Eton.

To be able to properly analyse the laws, I've split them into different groups. It is important to understand how the laws relate to the game being played – what a law is saying to the player. Here we are not looking at the reasons for why the laws exist, just the different types that do exist. I have given some examples from the 1845 Rules of Football at Rugby School booklet and the 1862 Rugby School Rulebook. I've identified the following types of laws that exist:

1) KNOWLEDGE – Identifying the location, personnel and equipment to be used in the game. Explaining the terminology used in the set of rules/laws and the way in which a game is to be played.

1862 – Introduction – *"Football is played on a large level field or piece of ground, near either end of which is erected a goal, composed of two upright posts eighteen feet high, with a crossbar placed ten feet from the ground."* – JMRB096

1845 – *"xxxii. – At a big-side, the two players highest in the School shall toss up."* – FORU016

1862 – *"16 – FIRST OF HIS SIDE is the player nearest the ball on his side."* – JMRB100

1862 – *"45 – The walk in front of the Headmaster's House, leading to the Barby Road is in goal."* – JMRB101

2) ACTION – Directing an action that is to take place during the game.

1845 – *"vi. – KICK OFF FROM MIDDLE must be a place."* – FORU009

1862 – *"A PLACE KICK is kicking a ball after it has been placed on the ground, in a small nick, made by the heel of the placer."* – JMRB099

1862 – *"3 – FAIR CATCH – is a catch direct from the foot, or a knock on from the HAND of the opposite side."* – JMRB099

1845 – *"xviii. – A player having touched the ball straight for a tree, and touched the tree with it, may drop from either side if he can, but the opposite side may oblige him to go to his own side of the tree."* – FORU012

3) AIM – Identifying the aim or object of a game: to score goals, *etc.*

1862 – Introduction – *"The object of the game is to kick the ball over the adversary's goal, which can be done either by dropping a goal or placing a goal: the former in the course of a game, and by any player of the opposite side who may happen to have the ball in his hands; the latter only after a touch down in goal."* – JMRB096

4) RESTRICTION – Creating boundaries for the actions, general play or other possible problems.

"viii. – RUNNING IN is allowed to any player on his side, provided he does not take the ball off the ground, or take it through touch." – FORU009

"xi. – No player being off his side shall hack, charge, run in, touch the ball in goal, or interrupt a catch." – FORU010

Lastly, rules and laws may be a combination of these categories. The two below tell players what they can and cannot do:

ACTION & RESTRICTION

1845 – *"ix. – Charging is fair, in case of a place-kick, as soon as a ball has touched the ground; in case of a kick from a catch, as soon as the player's foot has left the ground and not before."* – FORU009

1862 – *"20 – Though it is lawful to hold any player in a maul, this holding does not include attempts to throttle, or strangle, which are totally opposed to all the principles of the game."* – JMRB100

In the columns below I have tried to compare laws relating to similar subjects within the games, so that if Football at Eton is the parent game of Football at Rugby, it will become apparent because of the similarities in the laws. If one of the columns is blank it is because I can find no law covering a similar subject. Where the laws do cover similar subjects we need to look at whether these laws correspond to knowledge, actions, aims and/or restrictions of the games.

Subject	RUGBY 1845	ETON 1847
CATCHING	FAIR CATCH – A fair catch is a catch direct from the foot. (ACTION)	
CONDUCT	That all fellows not following up be strictly prohibited from playing any game in goal, or otherwise conducting themselves in any way which shall be deemed prejudicial to the interests of their side. (RESTRICTION)	
OFF-SIDE / POSITIONING	A player is off his side if the ball has touched one of his own side behind him, until the other side touch it. (KNOWLEDGE) No player being off side shall kick the ball in any case whatever. (RESTRICTION) No player being off his side shall hack, charge, run in, touch the ball in goal, or interrupt a catch. (RESTRICTION)	No player, if behind before the ball, may kick it up, or carry it to one of his own side to touch, but must leave it, where it stopped. (RESTRICTION) A player is considered to be sneaking when only three, or less than three of the opposite side are before him and may not kick the ball. (KNOWLEDGE)

	A player when off his side having a fair catch is entitled to a fair knock on, and in no other case. (ACTION) A player being off his side shall not touch the ball on the ground, except in touch. (RESTRICTION) A player being off his side cannot put on his side himself, or any other player, by knocking or throwing on the ball. (RESTRICTION) FIRST OF HIS SIDE is the player nearest the ball on his side. (KNOWLEDGE)	
HANDLING	A KNOCK ON – Distinguished from a throw on, consists in striking the ball on with arm or hand. (KNOWLEDGE) No player may stop the ball with anything but his own person. (ACTION & RESTRICTION)	Hands may only be used to stop the ball, or touch it when behind. The ball must not be carried, thrown, or struck by the hand. (ACTION & RESTRICTION)
ROUGE		A rouge is obtained by touching the ball first, after it has been kicked behind. (KNOWLEDGE) No player may run behind the goal sticks before the ball be kicked behind, either to prevent, or obtain a rouge. (RESTRICTION) Should the player, who has prevented the rouge have been

		behind before the ball, a player of the opposite side may touch it, and claim a rouge. (ACTION) If the ball go behind the goal sticks and without being touched, be kicked before them again, any player of the opposite side, if he can touch it first, may claim a rouge. (ACTION) If the ball be kicked behind by a cool kick, that is, when no one of the opposite side be bullying the kicker, No rouge, whoever touched it, can be obtained. (RESTRICTION) If a rouge be obtained before the time for leaving off expires, and the time expires, before the rouge is finished, the said rouge must be played out, until either a goal be obtained, or the ball be kicked outside the side sticks, or behind the goal sticks. (KNOWLEDGE) No rouge, or goal obtained after the time expires is admissible, except in the case of rule 16. (KNOWLEDGE) A rouge may be obtained by touching the ball, when on the line of the goal sticks. (ACTION)
KICK OFF	KICK OFF FROM MIDDLE, must be a place. (ACTION)	At the expiration of half time, goals must be changed, and a bully formed in the middle.
KICK OUT	KICK OUT must not be from more than ten yards of goal if	

	place-kick, not more than twenty-five yards, if a punt, or , drop, or knock on. (ACTION & RESTRICTION)	
KICKING	If a player take a punt when he is not entitled to it, the opposite side may take a punt or drop, without running if the ball has not touched two hands. (RESTRICTION)	
CRAWLING		No crawling on the hands and knees, with the ball between the legs is allowed. (RESTRICTION)
CHARGING A KICK	CHARGING is fair, in case of a place-kick, as soon as a ball has touched the ground; in case of a kick from a catch, as soon as the player's foot has left the ground, and not before. (ACTION & RESTRICTION)	
TOUCH	A player may not in any case run with the ball in or through touch. (RESTRICTION) No agreement between two players to send the ball straight out shall be allowed on big side. (KNOWLEDGE) A player touching the ball of his side must throw it straight out. (ACTION)	The ball is dead when outside, or in line with the side sticks, and must not be kicked. (KNOWLEDGE) When the ball is dead, it must be thrown in, or a bully formed parallel to the place where it stopped: these, are to take place alternatively. (ACTION) If the ball bounds off a bystander or any other object, outside the line of the side sticks, it may be kicked immediately on coming in. (ACTION) If the ball, when kicked out,

		bounds from any object without coming in, it must be put in parallel to the place, where it struck that object. (ACTION)
TACKLING	CONTACT – A player standing up to another may hold one arm only, but may hack him or knock the ball out of his hand if he attempt to kick it, or go beyond the line touch. (ACTION & RESTRICTION) No player may be held, unless he is himself holding the ball. (RESTRICTION) No hacking with the heel, or above the knee, is fair. (RESTRICTION) No player but the first on his side may be hacked, except in a scrimmage. (RESTRICTION)	
TREES & MISC	A player having touched the ball straight for a tree, and touched the tree with it, may drop from either side if he can, but the opposite side may oblige him to go to his own side of the tree. (ACTION) The discretion of sending into goal rests with the heads of sides or houses. (KNOWLEDGE) No player may wear projecting nails or iron plates on the heels or soles of his shoes or boots. (RESTRICTION) Nobody may wear cap or jersey	

	without leave from the head of his house.	
INJURY		If a player shall have begun the game and shall be hurt, or otherwise disabled from going on, no substitute may take his place. (KNOWLEDGE)
FALLING		The bully, or rouge must be broken, immediately a player falls on the ball and formed anew. (KNOWLEDGE) If a player falls on a rouge, or a bully, although not on the ball, and calls 'man down': or calls for 'Air', the said Bully or rouge must be broken, and formed anew. (KNOWLEDGE)
GOALS	All matches are drawn after five days, but after three if no goal has been kicked. (KNOWLEDGE) All little sides the goals shall be four paces wide, and in kicking a goal the ball must pass out of the reach of any player present. (KNOWLEDGE)	The goal sticks are to be seven feet out of the ground: a goal is gained when the ball is kicked between them provided it be not over the level of the top of them. (KNOWLEDGE) The space between each goal stick is to be eleven feet. (KNOWLEDGE) When a rouge has been obtained the ball must be placed one yard from the centre of the goals: and no player is to touch the ball, or let it rest against his foot, until the player, who obtained the rouge, has kicked the ball himself. (KNOWLEDGE & RESTRICTION)

		One goal outweighs any number of rouges, if each party has an equal number of goals, that party wins, which has the majority of rouges in addition to the goals. If no goals are obtained, the game Is decided by rouges. (KNOWLEDGE)
RULES OBSERVANCE	Heads of sides, or two deputies appointed by them, are the sole arbiters of all disputes. (KNOWLEDGE)	To prevent dispute it is better to appoint, before the game begins, two umpires: one chosen by each party, and a referee to be agreed on by both parties, where decisions, if the umpires differ, is to be final. It will be the duty of the umpires to enforce the rules: to decide on disputes that arise: to break a rouge, or bully, when necessary, and to see fair play for both parties. (KNOWLEDGE)

Looking at the above two sets of rules, there is no real common ground apart from the offside laws. The terminology in particular is very different. Rouges, bullies and sneaking at Eton, *vs.* scrimmage, fair catch and knock-on at Rugby. The common denominator as far as the terminology goes is the goal, but it's a different tye of goal: in Rugby it's over the bar and at Eton it's between the posts. We do find some more common ground in the form of place kicks in the memories of older players. In the 'Memories of Eton Sixty Years Ago' by Arthur Campbell Ainger:

"The most important alteration in the rules of the game, both in the Field and at the Wall, has been the curtailment of the privileges of the "behinds." Formerly they might catch the ball, deposit it on the ground, and so kick it. An adroit behind would catch the ball on his left hand and deposit it on his right, or vice versa, to the confusion of his adversaries. This has been stopped altogether in the Field and to a great extent at the Wall." – AAME166

Whilst at Rugby School, according to M.H. Bloxam:

"... caught the ball in his arms. This being so, according to the then rules, he ought to have retired back as far as he pleased, without parting with the ball, for the combatants

on the opposite side could only advance to the spot where he had caught the ball, and were unable to rush forward till he had either punted it or had placed it for someone else to kick, for it was by means of these placed kicks that most of the goals were in those days kicked, but the moment the ball touched the ground, the opposite side might rush on." – ORSR009

In both cases, after catching the ball, players had to place the ball on the ground to kick it. In the Eton game *"an adroit behind"* it seems would catch the ball one handed, then swap hands and kick it. The 1845 Football at Rugby School Rules (law v. – try at goal) mention *"even though it touch two hands",* which leads me to believe that at some earlier stage in the game catching one handed must have been the norm. The difficulty in analysing the laws of the developmental stages of the games is that the rules were verbal and so no records exist.

For Football at Eton to be the parent sport of Football at Rugby School, Eton Football would have had to have been played at Rugby School and the game would have had to have evolved of its own accord. My belief is that there is not enough common ground between the 1845 Football at Rugby Rules and the 1847 Football at Eton rules for it to be a real possibility. Not only are there differences in the natures of the games, but the terminology is almost completely different. The term 'goal' was used across several forms of school and folk football (MSAF279) so it cannot be regarded as being uniquely common to both of these codes of school football. There is some common ground with respect to place kicks and the emphasis on offside rules, as well as possibly one handed catching, so it is quite possible that Eton Football may have played some part in the origin of Football at Rugby School.

Although the Lower College game looked to be the most similar to Football at Rugby School, with the use of trees as goals, with no further information on the Lower College game at hand, we are forced to assume that the nature of the Lower College game was similar to the Field Game, but with the terminology and the goals being the difference.

I started this Chapter by saying that there were two possible options for Football at Rugby School to have started as a 'created sport'. We looked in detail at the Eton option, but we haven't looked at the possibility of a group of masters and/or boys at Rugby School drawing up plans for a game. It's a possibility but I think an unlikely one. If a group at the school had invented the game then surely they themselves or their contemporaries would have sung their praises for evermore. I refer again to Bloxam's notes on the handed down traditions at the school:

"At this time boys not unfrequently continued at School ten or even twelve years, and traditions of a longer date were handed down than at the present time, keeping remembrance of any stirring event alive." – MBRN087

SUMMARY – The earliest known date for Football at Rugby School was 1803–1806. We have undertaken research through the memoirs of the former pupil Charles Apperley and moved the earliest known date back to 1783 during the headmastership of Thomas James and at the time of former pupil turned writer Walter Savage Landor. James introduced the Eton education system into Rugby School in 1778. We've looked at the history of Eton Football and found that it pre-dates Thomas James' arrival at Rugby School by at least 12 years, so it's a possibility that Eton Football is the parent game of Football at Rugby School. We've analysed the rules of the two games and compared Football in the Field at Eton (the Field Game) to Football at Rugby School. We have decided that it is unlikely that Football at Rugby School descended from Eton Football and that it is equally unlikely that the game was invented by a group of Rugby School boys and/or masters.

CONCLUSION – It's possible that Football at Rugby School was a 'created game' and it's unlikely but not impossible that Football at Eton is its parent game.

FOOTNOTE – I'm fed up with songs, let's play a game. I'm going to call it sumspeed. The first one to multiply 77 x 77 and get the correct answer is the winner. The answer is 5939, I win. I think I could become world champion, what do you think? We could start by organizing a tournament with regional qualifiers leading up to a final which should take place in Sumderland. A bad joke, I know, let's move on…………..

CHAPTER 9 – WAS FOOTBALL AT RUGBY SCHOOL BORN THERE?

AIM – To look at the possibility that Football at Rugby School was born at the school and that it started of its own accord without any influence from external sources.

Children in a healthy environment like the playing fields of Rugby School will adapt to their environment and improvise with the things around them to have fun. It's the natural thing to do. What do you think would happen if you threw a ball of any shape or size onto a field of 150 boys at Rugby School? Even if they didn't know what it was, the boys would have been powerless to ignore it, instinct would have taken over and some sort of game would have ensued.

Let's look at the first set of laws laid down in 1845 at Rugby School:

"That all fellows not following up be strictly prohibited from playing any game in goal, or otherwise conducting themselves in any way which shall be deemed prejudicial to the interests of their side." – FORU004

The fellows who were not following up were the young boys stuck on the goal line, supposedly keeping the goal, but the goal was over the crossbar and too high for even the tallest boys to stop the ball. Unless of course they climbed onto the crossbar, which is why in the 1846 laws rule xix states:

"It shall be a goal if the ball goes over the bar (whether it touch or no) without having touched the dress or person of any player; but no player may stand on the goal bar to interrupt it going over." – ORSR030

If we think back to the evolution of a game, we'll see that these two laws are solving problems. The 'no games in goal' rule was introduced because the boys keeping goal had very little to do, so they invented games and things to do while the main game was going on.

"Whilst keeping goal and immediate attention was not required, games were often played by juniors, an old glove, stuffed with leaves, serving as a substitute for a football." – MBRN074

These games were probably far more interesting for the boys and they most likely forgot about the main game; so when they were called upon to make a play in the main game their minds were likely elsewhere. The 'no player may stand on the crossbar' rule was probably a result of a player or players having done this during a game, and so the rule was likely introduced to avoid a repetition of this dangerous act. It appears in the 1846 rules but not in the 1845 version, so we can assume that this happened between these dates. Once a game has a set of written rules, it's far easier to track its evolution with respect to the aims and actions of the players. This can be done through the rules and the memories of the players. Looking at the evolution of a game before the first set of written rules, however, is a bit trickier. We have to rely solely on any available reminiscences of the personnel involved. With Football at Rugby School, we can be thankful to the Old Rugbeian Society Report of 1897 for recording the memories of those who played the game before the first set of written rules were put in place. This gives us some insight into how the game was played in 1813, by Matthew Bloxam, and by others in the years leading up to the first written rules of 1845.

As we stated previously, the key to rugby football is the crossbar – the aim of kicking the ball over it and not under it. With this in mind I ask myself, has the origin of rugby football been under our noses the whole time and we just haven't seen it? Were Marshall, Shearman and the ORS toying with us? Let's look at the picture of the Close at Rugby School on the first page of Marshall's book:

THE CLOSE, RUGBY SCHOOL.

Notice anything familiar in the picture? - (FMRU001)

I'm not sure how old this picture is, but imagine those trees 50 years earlier. They'd be a lot smaller and would look just like the rugby posts on the right.

Are rugby posts the shape that they are because they were originally two trees standing together? Or maybe it's that one post represents one tree, the crossbar represents a branch and the other post is just a support for the crossbar? Look at how many trees there are on the Close at Rugby School in this painting and look at where the posts are in the white circle. They are right in front of the trees. Is this because the trees grew too tall and the posts were placed next to where the original goals were?

There was no Webb Ellis legend that survived at Rugby School but there are legends about the trees in Rugby School Close.

TREEN'S TREE – In Bloxam's 1880 account he talks about the 'famous Treen's Tree' that was felled in 1818 to make way for the chapel. It can be seen on the left-hand side of this 1809 illustration of the Close:

THE SCHOOL BUILDINGS FROM THE CLOSE, 1809.

'Treen's Tree' warranted a chapter of its own in 'Rugby – The School and its Neighbourhood', which was compiled from the edited writings of Matthew Bloxam. The school antiquarian opens the chapter with:

"To old Rugbeians up to the year 1818 no object in the School Close was of more interest than the famous elm, yclept "Treen's Tree," the site of which is now occupied by the western portion of the Chapel. It was the monarch of the elms in the Close..." – MBRN092

According to HC Bradby (HCBR088), Treen's Tree was named after the Treen family who held the farmyard in which it stood.

THREE TREES – These were part of the original Bigside (pitch).

"To a later generation the best known trees were a little group of three large elms, called the "Three Trees," which stood a little apart from their neighbours, about the middle of the ground as it was before the last addition; they were within the limits of the

football ground, and many a Rugbeian can still remember bruising himself against them; two of the three fell in 1881, but the remaining one retained the name, no longer applicable, till it shared the same fate in 1895." – HCBR088

TREES IN THE RULES – *"Rule xviii. – A player having touched the ball straight for a tree, and touched the tree with it, may drop from either side if he can, but the opposite side may oblige him to go to his own side of the tree."* – FORU012

CLIMBING TREES – Edmund Lally, aged 12, died in a fall from a tree which he had climbed to sit and read (MBRN097).

ROLLER TREE – In the second chapter of Marshall's book, Guillemard says "... *no trace is left of the Roller Tree which trespassed on the field of play on the Barby Road side of the ground."* (FMRU016).

CASE'S GALLOWS – *"Nor must we forget the tree that helped to form Case's Gallows, a peculiar goal set up in his school days by the present Waynflete Professor of Moral Philosophy at Oxford in which the cross-bar was formed by a horizontal branch of a tree which met the short arm of the "gallows". It stood between Old Bigside and the Chapel Piece."* – HCBR089

Although Case's Gallows were named as such after a post Webb Ellis Rugbeian, it shows that the boys were in the habit of using tree branches as crossbars. Case attended Rugby School 1858–1863 and the branches were most likely used as crossbars at 'puntabout', which was the term used by the boys for a 'practice session'.

Kids love trees – climbing them, running around them and using them as targets. Look again at the goalposts; the crossbar is the key. It is very easy to imagine that the original crossbar would have been the branch of a tree. If you look again at the map in the 1895 report you can see that the 'three trees' had a fence running through them. Was this fence the original reason why the ball was kicked over the branch rather than through the trees?

STREET FOOTBALL IN RUGBY TOWN

Let's go back to the time when Rugby School had no playground and was located in the middle of Rugby town. Some form of street football was played in the town of Rugby in the mid eighteenth century but it didn't survive. To quote from Jennifer Macrory's book:

"The Rugby game in particular has been regularly portrayed as a survival of 'primitive' football, generally on the grounds that carrying the ball is permitted. Certainly football was played in the town of Rugby in the middle of the eighteenth century. The Constable's books indicate that New Year's Eve rather than Shrove Tuesday brought football trouble to Rugby, and the entry for 31 December 1743/4 reads 'Pd Baxter for

Crying no football play in ye street, 2d'. Whatever form this local game may have taken it certainly did not result in the direct translation of the carrying game to the playing fields of the school, where the game played at the turn of the century distinctly forbade running with the ball." – JMRB014

The Constable's book says *"Pd Baxter for Crying no football play in ye street, 2d"*. It says nothing about running with the ball; it just says 'football'. If we refer back to Shearman and his different types of football, and to Routledge who refers to everything as football, we know that many different forms of football existed and we just don't know what type of football this was. We don't even know if it was a game of football; it could just have been a group of people playing and kicking a ball back and forth to each other. Neither does it say that this was an annual event: it could have been that a group of adults or kids had been playing football in the street every day since just before Christmas that year and that they had smashed so many windows that the constable decided he'd better do something about it – he paid the town crier to cry 'no football play in ye street' and if anybody did he'd have just cause to arrest them because they were warned.

Let's have a look at what was happening at Rugby School in 1743. It was without a playground and had just seen an influx of boarders after the appointment of a new master, Rev. Thomas Crossfield, in 1742. This is what Bloxam said about that period at Rugby School:

"In 1742, on the resignation of the Rev. John Plomer, the Rev. Thomas Crossfield was elected master to succeed him, and no one ever came to preside over the school with a greater prestige. In the first year of his mastership, fifty-three boys were admitted to the School, two only of whom were town boys. Of the remainder, one half were from the neighbouring county of Northampton, the other half from different parts of the kingdom. The expectations of a brilliant school career were frustrated by the early death, after a brief tenure of office, of Mr. Crossfield, in the thirty-third year of his age. The rush of scholars to Rugby during the early part of Mr Crossfield's mastership exceeded the number that could be accommodated in the Master's house, and accommodation had consequently to be found in the town; and it was during Mr Crossfield's mastership that I first find boarding houses alluded to..." – MBRN057

With the school building dilapidated, it's unlikely that any more pupils could have been accommodated under Crossfield and in 1744 only four pupils entered into the school. Of the 51 boarders who entered in 1742 I have identified at least four from the Rugby School Register who would have been very likely to have spent the Christmas period of 1743 at their boarding house in Rugby: Thomas Page, who was an orphan, and Thomas & John Brewster and Thomas Gibbs, all of whom were 'Barbadoes'. I'm assuming that this was a misspelling of Barbados, which was a British colony at the time. For these last three it would have taken them months rather than weeks to travel home and back again.

These four could have been our football players and there may even have been more boarders residing at Rugby over Christmas and the New Year. If we refer back to Apperley and his saturnalia comment, just 45 years after this date, we get an idea of what these boys were like. I'd say that it is quite probable that they were involved in playing football on the street.

So is this then the origin of Rugby Union? It's possible, but very unlikely. If these boys played football and developed a game with rules and that game evolved into the same one when the school moved seven years later and that game was still the same game that evolved into the one that Matthew Bloxam was playing, then yes, it is the origin. The boys of Rugby School may have played street football in 1743 but there is no record of that game or play having survived. If it had then I think there would have been mentions of arrests for 'football play' in the Constable's books.

If these boys had footballs they might have taken them to the churchyard where they were reprimanded by the rector for playing there. Perhaps they took balls out to the fields surrounding Rugby and developed a game there? Or perhaps they just put the ball in a cupboard and forgot about it? The school moved in 1750 to its new location – a manor house with grassy fields and trees. If the ball then came out of the cupboard we now have all of the ingredients needed for the birth of Rugby Union.

The term 'puntabout' appears at a later date in Rugby School folklore. This is where the boys kicked the balls back and fore to each other. Was 'puntabout' an early form of training, or was it the early form of Football at Rugby School? Let's explore the possibility that it was the latter.

Let's invent a game...........

Location = Rugby School Close, trees

Location + personnel = Rugby School Close, trees, two boys

Location + personnel + equipment = Rugby School Close, trees, two boys – one of whom is a butcher's son who brings a pig's bladder to school

Location + personnel + equipment + action = Rugby School Close, trees, two boys, a pig's bladder, punting the pig's bladder back and fore to each other

Location + personnel + equipment + action + aim = Rugby School Close, trees, two boys, a pig's bladder, punting the pig's bladder over a fence and a tree branch before the other boy punts it back. (They have developed an aim; this is 'puntabout').

The pig's bladder looks to be too light and one of the almsmen who helped with the move to the new school sees that the boys are having problems with it and remembers where the football is. He gives it to the boys who welcome the heavier pig's bladder encased in leather. More boys join in, with two then three a side. Charlie decides that it would be a good idea if when the ball went over the branch, the kicking team would score a point. The team with the most points at the end of play is the winning team. A game is born and we have:

Location + personnel + equipment + action + aim + verbal rules = game

It's now time for the game to evolve. To do this we need to:

1. Solve any problems that occur (problem solved)

2. Take opportunities to enhance the game wherever possible (enhancement made)

Charlie's team keep losing because Huw can't kick straight but he notices that Billy on the other side drops the ball more often than not, so Charlie, who is senior to the other boys, makes up the rule that if the receiving team catch the ball cleanly without it touching the ground then that point doesn't count. (Enhancement made)

Charlie leaves the school but most of the other boys remain and of the new intake there are 13 players who want to join in. The new players are shared amongst the teams and the game continues, but players keep bumping into each other and a number of injuries occur. The ground churns up and is muddy on one side only, while the other side remains firm and dry. Several of the boys on that side have slipped, fallen over and were punished for bringing mud into the schoolroom. Mike, the new senior boy amongst the players, decides that all of the boys apart from two catchers, one from each team, should move to the dry side and that the catchers still need to take the ball cleanly and then throw the ball back under the branch to the kickers. Kicks would then be taken alternately by each side. (Problem solved)

Specialist play starts to take shape. The best catchers from each side remain on the muddy side. Mike notices that the catcher in his team is not as good as the other team's catcher, so he makes up the rule that once a player has caught the ball he must rotate with other players in his team and must not become a catcher again until everyone else has had a go. (Enhancement made)

Huw remains a weak kicker, so Mike details a group of 20 fags to stand in strategic points so that if the ball goes astray from Huw's boot then they can bring it back into play quickly. (Problem solved)

Ten more senior boys turn up and want to play. The new boys are all from School House, making 24 seniors in total. Mike complains and tells them that there is not enough room for any more players. Ben, who wishes to join, is more senior in the school than Mike, so he tells him that they will join in and that they will all play in a bigger area and also use the branch of a different tree about 20–30 yards away. The catchers split up and move to the different trees. The ten new boys want to stay together so they make up one team and replace the catcher with one of their own. It's now ten School House boys against 14 of the rest of the school. One of the School House boys has an injured leg so they revert to having only a single catcher and they offer the option to the other team. (Problem solved)

As the nature of the game has changed with the multiplication of the 'goals', several problems occur immediately and are subsequently fixed.

The School House goals are at an angle and the branch (crossbar) is higher than that of the other goals, so the rest find it more difficult to kick the ball over the branch to score a goal. Four fags are detailed to hold up a tall broken branch at a better angle and it is agreed that the ball has to clear the top of this post to constitute a goal. (Problem solved)

The wind is blowing behind School House and they are leading 5–0. The rest are struggling to score a goal. Little Tommy kicks the ball and the wind catches it and takes it over the bar where it's caught by the School House catcher. School House claim a point but the rest dispute it because it wasn't a School House player who kicked the ball. The rest also complain about the wind and suggest that they change sides after every goal scored. Ben says OK. (Problem solved)

The game recommences with the teams changing sides after every goal. The catchers have to travel the furthest and the other players are annoyed at how long they are taking. Mike suggests to Ben that they do away with the catchers. The School House catcher is the better of the two but the other catcher is taking an age to cross over, so Ben agrees that it's a good idea. A point is once again awarded when the ball crosses over the branch. (Problem solved)

The four fags holding the goalposts get bored and start to mess around with their post. It falls on one of the boys and injures his shoulder. The headmaster wants to know how this happened and decides that post holding is too dangerous. He orders a local carpenter to build a set of posts that look like the original trees and has them installed at the correct angle. The carpenter erects the posts while the boys are in lessons but he couldn't find anyone to tell him at what distance to place the posts from the original trees. He is in a rush and has no idea how the game is played so he places them at a distance of 120 yards. The boys arrive to play and are astounded at the distance between the goals. Immediately they crowd around each other and begin a discussion on how to overcome this problem. It is decided that a player can kick the ball to his own player to advance the ball forward towards the opponent's goalposts. If the ball was caught then the next player could also kick it forward. But if the ball hit the floor then it was turned over and the other side could kick to advance. The game is still non-contact. The team without possession is not allowed to challenge for the ball – they must wait until the ball is dropped before they can claim it. (Problem solved)

Spring arrives and the goalposts, which on one side are trees, have heavy foliage and the ball keeps getting stuck in the trees. It is decided by the eldest boys, who have made a committee of 4 to adjudicate on the rules of the game, that the ball should be kicked off the floor because of the lower trajectory of flight. Therefore, when the ball is caught by a player who thinks that he can score a goal, he puts the ball down, retreats and attempts a kick at goal. (Problem solved)

The senior boys are chatting over lunch. As a group they have become dissatisfied with the game in general and the lack of action during matches. They discuss the nature of the game and how it seems that the team without the ball has nothing to do except watch as the other team progresses upfield. They want to look at ways in which both teams can be competing at the same time. They decide on a radical change. They decide that nobody from the same team can be in front of the player who kicks the ball. Players must follow up from behind the kick and try to catch the ball. This is to be called a fair catch. When a player makes a fair catch, he marks the ground where he caught the ball. The opposing team then stands on the mark and the 'fair catcher' retreats and kicks the ball again. The opposing team is allowed to contest for the fair catch but must not impede the player from the kicking side. A new pattern of play emerges. The kicker punts the ball high so that his 'followers' are able to cover more ground while the ball is in the air. If the ball hits the ground first or is dropped by the team in possession then it is turned over. If a defending player touched the ball last before it hit the ground then the attacking team keeps possession and makes their mark at that point. (Enhancement made).

The game is played in this way until the end of term. The boys return home for the summer, before coming back for the Michaelmas term. A new senior boy, Arthur, joins and numbers have been reshuffled over the summer period and it's now 17 School House boys against 28 from the rest of the school (including Arthur) with about 50 fags dotted around the touchlines and goal lines as ball boys. These fags mark the out of bounds areas but have no allegiance to either team. Arthur is a big kicker; he starts by following the previous strategy of kicking the ball high but then changes his mind and starts to kick for length rather than height because his team are only catching a low percentage of the kicks. The ball is quite often coming to rest near or beyond the opposition goal line before the defending team pick it up and kick it back. School House are continually losing distance because their kickers are not as powerful as Arthur. Ben (in his last year) suggests to the other senior boys that if the ball is on the floor then players are allowed to hit it with their hands or kick it forward towards the opposition goal in order to gain ground and keep the game in motion. The fair catch principle still stands if the ball is caught directly from a kick or a bounding ball. The kicker still makes a mark, and retires while the opposition advances to the mark. But if the ball is rolling or close to the floor then it must only be kicked or propelled forward with the hand; it is not allowed to be picked up. The other boys agree. (Enhancement made).

The game becomes more competitive with the introduction of kicking the ball on the floor and even fewer goals are scored. Attempts at goal are taking too long as a player has to catch the ball, place it, retire, then kick it. The game has developed a good tempo and levels of fitness amongst the boys are starting to improve. The senior boys want to maintain this tempo and bring in a rule that catchers are not allowed to kick at goal, and instead they must place the ball and a 'following up player' must take the kick. As soon as the catcher places the ball and the ball touches the ground then the opposing team may rush forward to attempt a block of the kick. Timing is critical and kicks are regularly charged down. (Enhancement made).

The senior boys are discussing the rules at length during lunch again and because it is a nice dry sunny day they reconvene their discussion on the Island. There are now six of them and they work well together so they decide to give themselves a name: 'Bigside Levée'.

The game is now mainly a kicking and catching game; punts are both long and high and normally the catcher has little time to field the ball. When it is dropped, 20 or 30 boys set upon it immediately and try kicking it towards the opponent's goal. Not all of the boys join the scrummage; some stay out judiciously waiting for the ball to appear. The rules stay the same for a number of years and the natural tree goalposts are replaced by artificial posts. The pitch is lengthened and the trees are natural obstacles on the pitch that are incorporated into the set of verbal rules. Goals are now rarely scored and matches can go on for days without a score.

One day, as was usual, a boy caught the ball in his arms. This being so, according to the rules, he should have retired back as far as he pleased, without parting with the ball. The combatants on the opposite side could only advance to the spot where he had caught the ball. They were unable to rush forward until he had either punted it or had placed it for someone else to kick. This boy disregarded this rule, and upon catching the ball, instead of retiring backwards, rushed forwards with the ball in his hands towards the opposite goal. The Bigside Levée got together and passed a rule that if that happened again then the boy should be hacked over, that is, have his legs kicked out from under him. (Problem solved)

At the start of this process we had two boys with a ball and at the end we had a game with rules. The final action in this sequence, and I hope you recognized it, was the William Webb Ellis event. I wanted to include this to show that in this hypothetical game invented at Rugby School, he was not the inventor. The inventor of the game was Charlie because he devised the rule that made kicking over the crossbar the aim of the contest. In the evolutionary path, he had invented the game:

Location + personnel + equipment + action + aim + verbal rules = game

SUMMARY – We've seen that the boys of Rugby School may have played football as far back as in 1743. When the school moved to the Manor House, the Close had all of the ingredients needed to start the game of Football at Rugby School. If a ball had been thrown onto the Rugby School Close while the boys were playing, it's inconceivable that they would have ignored it. Some sort of play would have commenced immediately and then a game would eventually have been born. We have shown that the trees on the Close were probably involved at some early stage in the development of the game. We have also shown how a game could have started and we have suggested a potential theoretical link from that start to the earliest known form of the Football at Rugby School game. Therefore, we must agree that it is possible for the game of Football at Rugby School to have been born there between 1742 and 1809.

CONCLUSION – It is possible that Football at Rugby School was born there and if this is the case then the origin of Rugby Union can be placed at Rugby School.

FOOTNOTE – In an early draft of this chapter I included the word ambididdlemous but this somehow has been edited out. This word means the inability to tell left from right, there are thousands, maybe hundreds of thousands of people who can't tell their left from their right; you may be one of them. I just wanted to use the word in this book because it is one I made up about 15 years ago during a made up game in the swimming pool. People have started to use it, there was a discussion on Radio Scotland about it and someone has suggested it should be included in the Collins dictionary. The world needs this word, please use it, please tell your friends about ambididdlemous. Moving on and back to sumspeed, did you believe that 77 x 77 = 5939 without checking first? Because the answer is really 5919 and I was just showing you how easy it is to believe everything that you read. Before you had a chance to think about it, I moved you on by talking about a related subject and then changing the subject completely with a bad joke. Unless you were very thorough and checked, you would have assumed that I knew what I was talking about and believed that 5939 was the correct answer. That's how the Old Rugbeian Society got away with the report, because it was titled 'The Origin of Rugby Football'. Once people read the title and they were told that Bloxam had stated that the Webb Ellis event was the origin they believed that they were reading about the origin of Rugby Union, whereas we now know differently. Nobody checked what Matthew Bloxam had actually said. We've now checked to see if Football at Rugby School was 'created' or 'born' and found that it's possible that it could be either. When I was doing research for this book, at this point my money was on the boys of Rugby School having invented their own form of Football. But I'm not 100% happy with that theory. If the boys of Rugby School had invented the game then why hasn't Matthew Bloxam mentioned this. I think that we should be asking more questions about Bloxam, so let's do that.

CHAPTER 10 – DOES MATTHEW BLOXAM HOLD THE KEY TO THE ORIGIN OF FOOTBALL AT RUGBY SCHOOL?

AIM – To explore the writings of Matthew Bloxam more closely in order to see if there is any additional information that can be gathered relating to the origin of Rugby Union.

When I started writing this book it was only going to be a short article for www.world-rugby-museum.com so that I could explain how Webb Ellis had invented the game of rugby football. Writing a book about the origin of Rugby Union was not the aim. I only set out to understand the origin of the game. To do this I've had to take a closer look at sport in general and read a lot of books about Rugby Union and the public schools. I don't want to blow my own trumpet too hard but in playing sport I was reasonably successful. A lot of the time my victories or accomplishments were down to sheer hard work – in training, in researching methods of play or technique and finally in determination. I think that throughout my life I have developed an instinct for sport. This is why within a few minutes of picking up the 1897 Old Rugbeian Society report, I knew that the Webb Ellis event was not the origin of rugby, and when reading through Shearman and Marshall's books, I had the same feeling about folk football.

While I've been working on this book there is one name that keeps cropping up – Matthew Holbeche Bloxam. Particularly while I was writing the last few chapters of the book, my instinct clicked into overdrive when it came to Mr Bloxam. I knew that there was something wrong with his writings and with his published articles, but for a long time I just couldn't put my finger on it. Scratching my head and asking myself questions about Bloxam almost became a full time occupation.

Firstly, let's look at what Matthew Holbeche Bloxam says about himself:

"I consider myself in some respects as one connecting the past with the present. I have transacted business with a Rugbeian who entered Rugby School in the reign of George II. – 127 years ago. I entered Rugby School nigh 72 years ago, and left the School 64 years ago; but whilst I was at Rugby a retired Master of the School died who was born in 1718, early in the reign of George I., 167 years ago. The Rev Henry Holyoak was master of Rugby School in the boyhood of that old retired master, and Mr Holyoak was alive in the lifetime of a nephew of Lawrence Sheriff, the Founder of Rugby School. Now Lawrence Sheriff died 318 years ago; such is my knowledge of the past." – MBRN0xxxii

The above extracts and the two below are from the book 'Rugby – The School and Neighbourhood' – a compilation of Bloxam's papers and articles. This is what his brother John Rouse Bloxam says about him:

"Born at Rugby, May 12, 1805, dying at Rugby, April 24, 1888, living almost without a break at Rugby for those 83 years, the son of a Master at the school, the friend of generation after generation of Rugby boys and masters, Matthew Holbeche Bloxam was Rugbeian to the backbone. Nothing delighted him more in his later years than to gather round him a little circle of his friends among the boys in the School, and to recall to them, the folk of modern times, the Rugby of the far-off past; to tell them of the terrific combats and Homeric feasts, in which their predecessors, when the century was young, indulged; to describe the rude methods of football in those days, and the variations at times indulged in of hoops, marbles, and pegtops; to dwell on the memory of the friends of the past, and especially to tell of such of his contemporaries as were still surviving. Among the various records of the history of the School, few equal in interest the paper which Mr. Bloxam read before the Natural History Society in November, 1883, entitled "Personal Reminiscences of Rugby School as it was in 1813, 70 years ago"..." – MBRN0xix

The editor of the book, W.H. Payne, wrote:

"In an article on Rugby School, in the New Quarterly Magazine, October 1879, after some three pages of introductory matter, the writer says "In the history of the School itself, apart from its external growth, there is nothing known that is worth recording till

the year 1828, when Dr. Wooll was succeeded by Dr Arnold." This statement shows a somewhat limited range of vision. Mr Bloxam, himself one of the most distinguished Rugbeians of that earlier era, spent great part of his life in investigating and recording the history of the School previous to 1828. This book might indeed be called "Præ-Arnoldian Rugby." It will show that there were some things worth recording in that dim and distant past, and will, it is to be hoped, keep alive the memory, not only of the distinguished writer and antiquary, but of other good men and true, who adorned Rugby in her comparatively early days." – MBRN0pf.v

Bloxam was actually born in a Rugby School dames' house run by his father R.R. Bloxam, a master at the school. In the history of Rugby School there is only one person who could possibly lay claim to being a more through and through Rugbeian than Matthew Holbeche Bloxam O.R., F.S.A. and that's his father Rev. Richard Rouse Bloxam who was a pupil 1777–c1784, a master at the school from 1790 until 1827 and a 'fellow of the school' until his death in 1840 (MBRN0xvii).

Rev. Richard Rouse Bloxam
(image courtesy of Rugby School)

I read through the book of Matthew Bloxam's articles and papers about the town of Rugby and Rugby School and I came to the conclusion that he was obsessed with old churches. Why else would he write books on gothic architecture and write extensively about pews, galleries, monuments, ministers and monks and about who is buried where and who has donated items to the churches in and around Rugby. Eleven pages of the book are dedicated to Lutterworth Church and he dedicates several other pages to other churches in the area. Football at Rugby School is mentioned on occasion in the book but everything points to a man who goes to church to look around and see what it is made of.

Something was still not right. I came across another letter penned by him in the London Standard, this one in reply to a previous article that had stated that there were Old Rugbeians at a Rugby School event that had done 'battle at football' on the Close 25 years before. This letter is dated 22 October 1872, four years before his first mention of William Webb Ellis. Bloxam wrote about those who had played football on the Close 50 years earlier. The error in the original article is pretty innocuous but Bloxam is proud that he played on the Close and is stirred enough into writing a letter to correct the Standard:

"RUGBY SCHOOL FOOTBALL – TO THE EDITOR OF THE STANDARD

SIR, - In your article of this day on Rugby School, which will have been read with deep interest by many an old Rugbeian, you allude to "those who had fought the daily battle of football on the old close a quarter of a century since." May I be permitted to state that at least half a dozen old Rugbeians were present at the meeting on Sunday last, who had fought the battle of football on the old close upwards of half a century ago. Perhaps I may be allowed to mention names:- The Bishop of Rochester; C.M. Caldecott, Esq., J.P., of Holbrooke Grange, one of those whose uncle entered Rugby School upwards of 120 years ago; the Rev. E.M. Stanley, who officiated as chaplain to the Bishop of Rochester; two of my brothers, the Rev. Andrew Bloxam and the Rev. John Rouse Bloxam D.D.; and myself. There were then no distinctive badges of honour, bags or flannels; and caps, which are at the present day so eagerly contested for and dearly prized by Rugbeians, were unknown; but time has not effaced the feelings of attachment, veneration and affection which still exists amongst the surviving Rugbeians of half a century and more towards the old school at Rugby – Oct 22 – MATTHEW HOLBECHE BLOXAM." – LEVS18721023

When I read his other letters I realized that both the 1876 Standard letter and the Meteor article in response to the Times article were corrections to the remarks of others. Bloxam was pointing out errors that were appearing in print. Let's look at the 1876 Standard letter first.

"Permit an old Rugbeian, at school under the headmastership of Dr. Wooll, who resigned that office in the summer of 1828, to say a few words on the point in controversy in the present Rugby game. The running with the ball in one's hands is of no

great antiquity as regards Rugby, it has there originated within the last half-century." – LEVS18760226

And in 1880:

"A leading article in the Times newspaper, the leading journal of Europe, a few weeks past, on the Rugby School Football Rules and Play, as contrasted with the Association Rules, has prompted me to write a few words on the game of football, as played at Rugby in my time, 1813–1820…In the latter half year of 1823, some 57 years ago, originated, though without premeditation, that change in one of the rules, which more than any other has since distinguished the Rugby School game from the Association Rules… It was Football and not handball, plenty of hacking, but little struggling." – METR18801222

Bloxam's response to the Times letter was to show that he had played football. At that time, in the 1880s, the term football was becoming more and more associated with the Association game. It's obvious from his letters that Bloxam was an authority on the game and knew all about Football at Rugby School. That's why he was correcting articles and letters that appeared in the daily newspapers. He introduced the Webb Ellis story and he was very informative about football as he had played it between 1813 and 1821. He knew all about the rules and the dress of the players. Then it clicked that what was missing from the combined writings of Matthew Holbeche Bloxam was the origin of Football at Rugby School. He was a historian, so surely he would have been interested in when football had first come to Rugby School. So what I did next was to go back through the book 'Rugby – The School and the Neighbourhood' and I have listed mentions of most of his origin theories on various subjects below.

"…hence the origin of boarding houses." – MBRN002

Speaking of the 1797 Great Rebellion: *"Its origin was as follows."* – MBRN065

"When I first entered Rugby School a barbarous custom existed, which would hardly be permitted in these days, and the origin of which I am altogether unable to trace." – MBRN071

"From this custom originated the frequent pugilistic encounters which then took place…" – MBRN072

"Now the curious feature in this case was that there was no premeditation: the whole originated from an individual, and he not one of the leaders of the run." – MBRN088

Speaking of Swift, author of Gulliver's Travels, visiting the East Sheen playing field: *"Here Swift, the celebrated Dean of St Patrick's, was a constant visitor, and amidst these academic groves it is possible the idea of those celebrated travels of Captain Lemuel Gulliver may have originated."* – MBRN102

Of the no running forward with the ball rule: *"I have since ascertained that this change originated with a Town boy or Foundationer of the name Ellis, William Webb Ellis..."* – MBRN110

"In the latter half-year of 1823, some 57 years ago, originated though without premeditation, that change in one of the rules, which more than any other has since distinguished the Rugby School game from the Association rules." – MBRN109

Of Treen's Tree: *"I have failed in my endeavours to make out the origin of the name."* – MBRN093

About Mr Robert Dover's Olimpick Games upon Cotswold Hills: *"These games, if not the origin, were the precursors of our present athletic sports."* – MBRN111

"That honoured institution the Crick Run, though of no great antiquity, having been started considerably within the last 50 years, though its origin is now lost in oblivion..." – MBRN142

"Of this streamlet, a legend – the origin of which I have been unable to trace..." - MBRN147

"On the table land, over these fields, before the Rugby enclosure took place in 1774, the Rugby Races were run, and the second field from the road still retains the name of "Starting Post Close." When these races originated I know not; I can only trace them back to 1721." – MBRN152

About the Gunpowder Plot conspirators' meeting house: *"...not only is the tradition extremely vague, but I think I can point out the origin."* – MBRN150

About an arch in Bilton Church: *"Of the origin, progress, development and disuse of this rite, I have lately treated in a paper read by me..."* – MBRN169

"To the bloody hand of Ulster, then, we may look for the origin of the Legend of Lawford Hall, – a legend I can trace no higher than the middle of the eighteenth century." – MBRN189

"The remembrance of two of old time, Paschasius Radbertus, who raised or originated the great religious controversy of the ninth century..." – MBRN197

"This, no doubt, had originally a wooden door and lock to fasten it, but no traces of the door are now apparent." – MBRN205

"...how and when it originated, Bishop Jewel treats at length in "The Defence of the Apology of the Church of England,"..." – MBRN207

As we can see from the above examples, Bloxam has attempted to establish the origin of various subject matters. The Rugby School Athletic Sports he has attributed to Mr Robert Dover's Cotswold Olimpick Games. The Rugby Races he traced back to 1721, but says that he could not trace them back any further. He says that the running rule in football originated with Ellis. He was unable to identify the origin of the name 'Treen's Tree'. Bloxam was like all other 19th century historians and writers: they aspired to reach the dizzy heights of Charles Darwin and 'origin' was the buzzword of the day. Charles Darwin junior was even a pupil at Rugby School in the 1850s so it's possible that Bloxam rubbed shoulders with the great man himself. Bloxam wasn't frightened of pinpointing an origin or saying that he didn't know about something's origin or even guessing what the origin of a particular thing was. But of Football at Rugby School, its origin or any reference to it remains absent throughout the book.

Reference to the origin of Football at Rugby School isn't the only sporting origin missing. The origins of cricket and Eton Fives at Rugby School are notable absentees. I was surprised to learn from H.C. Bradby's 1900 history of the school that there were four Eton Fives courts in Rugby School (HCBR138 & 139). This was the last clue that I needed. Bloxam hadn't mentioned Eton Fives at all. He knew how football had arrived at Rugby School and the reason that he avoided telling anyone about it was because he didn't like it. He believed that the origin lay with Football at Eton School, which arrived during the headmastership of Thomas James and his remodelling of the school on the Eton system. Thomas James needed a prosperous school so he copied the successful Eton system of education, the five lessons a day, praeposters & fags, dames' boarding houses and he imported Eton's successful sports including cricket, football and fives. Matthew Bloxam knew this. His father, Richard Rouse Bloxam, had first entered the school in 1777 in the last intake of pupils before the start of James' reign. He left as an exhibitioner in about 1784, but was back again as a master in 1790 when the school was still under James' leadership. Like his son, Bloxam senior was a historian and it was he who penned the chapter on Rugby School in Nicholas Carlisle's 1818 book on the grammar schools of England and Wales. If James had introduced Eton Football at Rugby then Bloxam senior would have known because he was at the school both when James started and when he finished. He would have passed this information onto his son. If he hadn't have learnt it from his father, Matthew Bloxam would have learnt it from asking questions of other Old Rugbeians with whom he came into contact. As Payne said, he *"spent a great part of his life in investigating and recording the history of the School previous to 1828"*.

Matthew Bloxam was an honest man, which is why in his printed works you won't find any information whatsoever on the origin of Football at Rugby School. He simply doesn't volunteer this information. He knows how football arrived at the school but chooses to withhold the information, volunteering only the details about how football was played in his time, and doing so when he needs to correct the misconceptions of others. He wants people to know that he played 'football' and not 'rugby', which is how the game was becoming known. Rugby to him meant two things – his town and his school. He never played rugby: he played football and he always referred to it as such when he was talking about the game he played. When he needed to refer to the game of Rugby Union, he called it "*the present Rugby Football*" game – referring to Rugby, the school that he attended, and football, the game that he played there. He brought up the Webb Ellis story to prove that he was playing football and not handball.

Let me put you in a similar position to see how you react. Imagine that your father is in prison for manslaughter. He accidentally killed someone with a chainsaw when he was cutting down trees. He was messing around with the chainsaw; it slipped and cut an artery in his workmate's leg. He tried hard to stem the bleeding, performed first aid, called for help and did everything he could to save his mate's life. The court didn't see it that way, they focused only on his messing around and he was sentenced to 10 years in prison. Five years later you are on holiday and have met a group of people and you are all discussing the film the Texas chainsaw massacre. Someone in the group googles chainsaw deaths and they come across your father's story. The 'googler' starts to tell his story but then starts to invent information around the story. They say that your dad went on a rampage through a shopping centre, cutting people's arms and legs off, that he was an evil man and that he is in prison for life and that he deserves everything that he is getting. You love your dad; do you:

a) Stay silent?
b) Tell the correct the story?

If you are like me then my guess is that you'll plump for option b), and previously to that you wouldn't have volunteered any information about your dad being in prison at all. With Bloxam's writings I'd say that he is in a similar situation with Thomas James' Eton System. He doesn't mention James' introduction of the Eton system in the article on him that appears in 'Rugby – The School and Neighbourhood'. There is just one mention of Eton, and that was that Dr James was a former pupil there.

Remember his opening boast?

"Now Lawrence Sheriff died 318 years ago; such is my knowledge of the past." – MBRN0xxxii

Let's look again at what W.H.D. Rouse says in his 1898 history of Rugby School:

"James brought with him to Rugby Cambridge scholarship and Eton methods. We shall soon find not merely the tutorial system in full swing, and a body of præpostors served

by fags, but dames' houses, and other things and customs which speak of the same origin." – WRRS129

By other things is Rouse referring to sports – cricket, football and Eton Fives?

The good news for all future Rugbeians is that Eton Football was run by the boys; it was they who made up the rules and organized the games. The other good news is that the goal in Football at Eton is low – between the posts. It's only at Rugby School that we find the goal above the crossbar. We've already decided through the analysis of the rules that it's highly unlikely that Football at Eton was the parent game of Football at Rugby School. For Thomas James to have introduced Eton football to Rugby School, he would have had to have introduced some Eton schoolboys too to teach others the game and had this have happened then the terminology of the Eton game would have stuck.

THOMAS JAMES

If Thomas James were alive today he would be known as 'Thomas the Beast'. He loved nothing more than to flog and cane his pupils. 'Discipline' was his word. Whilst he was a pupil at Eton School 1761–1766 he wrote a whole pamphlet on the subject of Eton discipline. He had no interest in sport but he did recognize it as a necessary reward for good behaviour. 'Play' was his buzzword. In his pamphlet on discipline he mentions play 25 times, adding that *"it [would] encourage in the boys a spirit of Emulation."* (TJED001–012). It's likely that James tried to teach a form of Eton Football to the boys at Rugby but as the game was self-regulated by the players it quickly would have taken on a new course of evolution.

I think that this is what happened: either Thomas James or James Chartes turned up on the Close one day with a ball and said to the boys of the 6th form "this is a football and this is how we used to play football at Eton – we kicked the ball against the tree and that constituted a goal. If you are in front of the ball when it is kicked you are off-side. Use your fags to keep goal; that keeps them out of mischief. You (to the head of school) are in charge. Now play."

TERMINOLOGY OF THIS ORIGIN

Previously we stated that a sport can either originate from a birth or from a creation. This is not a birth; it is a type of creation but not a type that we've encountered so far. As was the case for the education system, Football at Rugby School was intended to be a copy of Football at Eton, so it was modelled on that game, as opposed to having broken away from or evolved directly from it. From this conclusion I think we can say that Football at Eton is a contributory game of Football at Rugby School and that Football at Rugby School was created as a model of Football at Eton.

We now find ourselves in a grey area. If the boys were playing a game modelled on Football at Eton, but not actually the same game that was being played at Eton, then were they playing Football at Rugby School or Football at Eton? We could refer back to the Rugby League precedent. The difference being though that Rugby League began as a sport with a governing body formed before the first game was played, whereas Football at Eton is a game and not a sport; however, the circumstances are similar enough to draw a comparison. We have decided already that the birth/creation of Rugby Union was when the goal moved to be above the crossbar, so I think that we should stick with that and call what the boys were playing an early developmental stage of Football at Rugby School. The origin of Rugby Union should be attributed to the very second that the aim of this game became such that the goal moved to be above the crossbar. The beginning of our timeline on the origin of Rugby Union now looks like this:

1778–1782 – Football at Rugby School, modelled on Football at Eton, began.

1783–c1790 – Earliest account of Football played at Rugby School, by Walter Savage Landor.

1778–1813 – Sometime between these dates the aim of the game changed to the distinctive feature of scoring a goal by kicking the ball above the crossbar. (Origin of Rugby Union)

1813 – MH Bloxam entered Rugby School and later provided the oldest account of how the game was played.

1823 – William Webb Ellis possibly cheated in a game that had a set of verbally agreed rules, giving rise to the possibility that running forward with the ball could be a feature of the game.

Circa 1830s – Running forward with the ball was allowed.

1841 – 'Running in' was allowed.

1845 – The first set of football rules were drawn up for Football at Rugby School. (Creation of Rugby School Rules)

Detailed research of the Rugby School trustees' books, Thomas James' letters and notes, Matthew Bloxam's archives and other Rugby School archives would be required to establish as to whether there is an exact date of origin available, but I would guesstimate this to be about 1780–1782. It's possible that the boys' enjoyment in smashing windows may have had a bearing on the origin of the sport and may explain why the goal is above the crossbar and not below it:

"A sort of Saturnalia, now I should hope abolished, followed the speeches. The last few days of the half-year were spent in all kinds of riotous excesses; no lessons were expected to be done, excepting after a manner chosen by the boys – that is to say, anyhow; and half of the windows of the school were broken…" – CALT149

Somehow I can't see the masters allowing pure vandalism to take place, where the boys would have just been picking up stones and throwing them through the windows. That would have been pretty dangerous for the people inside the school. For the boys to have been smashing windows, I think that there must have been an alternative explanation, perhaps one where they were playing cricket or a game of puntabout among the trees next to the school and they were accidentally (on purpose) smashing windows in the process.

SUMMARY – Matthew Holbeche Bloxam was an honest historian and he was painstakingly detailed in his research and his work. He must have known as to how football came to be played at Rugby School because his father would have known about the game and he was famed for his detailed research into the school's history. If he hadn't have known what the origin was, he would have said so or made an informed guess based on the available information. Matthew Bloxam kept quiet because he believed that its origins lay with the Eton game. It's most likely that Football at Rugby School was modelled on one of the forms of Eton Football. Football at Rugby School then evolved, as driven by the senior pupils. If this was indeed the case, we can consider the point of origin of Rugby Union to be to point in time when the goal changed to being over the crossbar during this evolution process. To establish the correct date of origin for Rugby Union, detailed research of Matthew Bloxam's and the Rugby School archives is required.

CONCLUSION – It's very probable that Football at Rugby School was modelled on one of the forms of Eton Football, most likely the Lower College Game. That game is therefore a contributing game to Football at Rugby School. The origin of Rugby Union is when the aim of Football at Rugby School became such that to score a goal the ball had to go over the crossbar. This may have been its aim at the outset.

FOOTNOTE – It's taken us a while but I believe we got there in the end. If I had to put a figure of probability on the above conclusion, I'd say it was a 98% certainty. This is just my personal view and I am just one man; you may think differently, or you may even know differently. If you do then I'd like you to challenge my opinions. This book is about understanding the origin of Rugby Union and we still haven't quite found exactly when the sport originated, so we should still keep asking questions and open this topic for discussion to the Rugby Union and sporting world. Once people have had the chance to read the book and digest its contents, if there are differing opinions then we should talk about them. With that in mind, in January 2017 I hope to start two Facebook groups.

Group 1 will be an open group where you can leave a message, introduce yourself, explain who you are and what your role in the sport is and point us towards any of your previous publications or thoughts. Then you should request to join Group 2. There are no rules as to who can or can't join Group 2, but we want to avoid time wasters or spectators joining the discussion group. You may be asked to add more information about yourself. Group 2 will be a closed group in which theories and information can be discussed between members.

I may be wrong with my conclusion. If I am, then hopefully this book will kick start a dialogue that can be continued using modern communication methods and in a few years time maybe we can publish another book or an article on the 'actual origin' of Rugby Union that is agreed by all. Links to the Facebook pages will be available on www.world-rugby-museum.com

CHAPTER 11 – THE ORIGIN AND EVOLUTION OF RUGBY UNION

AIM – To assign probabilities to the theories on the origin of Rugby Union that we have discussed in the preceding chapters and to summarise the evolution.

Rugby Union is a sport that can draw a line of direct evolution from its early developmental stage – the game of Football at Rugby School – to the present day, by looking at the sets of written laws that have been published over the years. The only aim of Football at Rugby School throughout its recorded history was to score a goal by kicking the ball over the crossbar by a place or drop kick. In the early days of the game, it's most likely that the crossbar was actually a tree branch. The goal continued to be the main aim of Rugby Union throughout its secondary developmental stage as Rugby School Rules, as well as during the first 108 years of its existence as the sport of Rugby Union, up until 1979. The goal is still the distinctive feature of the game of Rugby Union, as can be seen from the results of Rugby Union's showpiece event – the Rugby World Cup Final. The actual date of origin of the sport of Rugby Union is unknown, but can most likely be identified as the exact moment in the game of Football at Rugby School that the rule that the ball must go above the crossbar in order for a goal to have been scored was introduced. I believe this to have been circa 1780–1782.

The probabilities of the previously discussed theories for the origin of Rugby Union being the correct one, and the relevant related dates for each theory are as follows:

ORIGIN POSSIBILITY 1 – There is a very high probability that Thomas James and/or James Chartes showed or advised the boys of Rugby School how to play Eton Football, or how to play a game with a similar style to Eton Football, circa 1778–1782. This game immediately became Football at Rugby School because it was played in a different location with different personnel to Eton Football. The game was self-regulated by the boys and at some point in time its aim became 'to score a goal by kicking the ball over the crossbar'. It is that point in time, when this aim became a verbal rule that marks the origin of Rugby Union. The abundance of Elm Trees in the Rugby School Close gives me reason to believe that this would have occurred very early on in the evolution of the Football at Rugby School game and that it may even have been the aim at its outset. I believe the probability of this being the origin of Rugby Union to be very high, with the actual date of origin to be sometime between 1778 and 1812, but most likely between 1780 and 1782.

Correct terminology – There is a very high probability that the origin of Rugby Union lies at Rugby School between 1778 and 1812 during an early developmental form of the sport, termed Football at Rugby School. Football at Eton is a contributory sport of Football at Rugby School.

ORIGIN POSSIBILITY 2 – There is a low probability that between 1743 and 1776, the boys and/or masters at Rugby School invented the game of Football at Rugby School from scratch, either by birth or by creation. This took place without the direction of an Old Etonian or the influence of any other game. In the case of the 'birth', the origin lies with when the first rule was made. In the case of the 'created game', the origin lies with when a resolution to play the game was made, or if no resolution was made then the origin lies with when an agreement on the rules of the game was made. I believe the probability of either of these methods being the origin of Rugby Union to be low.

Correct terminology – There is a low probability that the origin of Rugby Union lies at Rugby School, circa 1743–1776, with the boys and/or masters having birthed or created an early form of the sport, termed Football at Rugby School.

ORIGIN POSSIBILITY 3 – It is extremely unlikely that before 1777 one or more pupils or masters introduced a type of folk football to Rugby School and taught it to the boys, or that a form of folk football arrived at Rugby School by some other means and developed into Football at Rugby School. To be considered as the origin of Rugby Union, the aim of this form of folk football must have been to score a goal by kicking the ball over the crossbar and between the posts and this must have been the aim of the game prior to it arriving at Rugby School. I believe the possibility of this being the origin of Rugby Union to be extremely unlikely.

Correct terminology – It is extremely unlikely that the origin of Rugby Union lies with a form of folk football.

Caveat – If you believe that a form of folk football is the origin of Rugby Union then you must be able to supply a clear evidence-based or potential theoretical pathway from that or those particular types of folk football to Football at Rugby School, proving that the main aim in that ancient form of folk football was to score a goal by kicking the ball over a crossbar.

OTHER – I believe that it is not possible that the origin of Rugby Union is something different to the above three possibilities.

SUMMARY OF THE EVOLUTION OF RUGBY UNION

Step 1 – LOCATION – Rugby School, trees or posts with a crossbar.

Step 2 – PERSONNEL – The pupils of Rugby School.

Step 3 – EQUIPMENT – Ball.

Step 4 – ACTIONS – Mainly kicking and catching the ball.

Step 5 – AIM – To score a goal a player had to kick the ball over the crossbar and between the posts.

Step 6 – GAME – A set of rules for Football at Rugby School are verbally agreed between the personnel.

The ORIGIN occurred between 1743 and 1812 – the moment that steps 5 and 6 became coexistent.

Step 7 – ORGANISED GAME – 1845 – First written rules of Football at Rugby School are put in place.

Step 8 – SPORT – 1862 – The first set of rules for the game of Football at Rugby School that could be played elsewhere, in places other than Rugby School, were put in place. The governing body was Rugby School and the sport was called Rugby School Rules

Step 9 – NATIONAL SPORT – 1871 – The Rugby Football Union was formed in order to govern the Rugby School Rules sport in England. This sport became known as Rugby Union

Step 10 – INTERNATIONAL SPORT – 1886 – The International Board was formed by members of the Scottish, Irish & Welsh Unions. This organisation is now called World Rugby and it is the governing body worldwide for the sport of Rugby Union

THE WILLIAM WEBB ELLIS EVENT

It is impossible that the William Webb Ellis event is the origin of Rugby Union. Even if the event happened, and there is an element of doubt as to whether or not it did, Football at Rugby School was already in place when Webb Ellis was playing it.

Correct terminology – The William Webb Ellis event is not the origin of Rugby Union.

Caveat – If you still believe that the Webb Ellis event is the origin of Rugby Union then you must be able to provide acceptable answers to the following questions:

What game was William Webb Ellis playing in 1822?

What game was William Webb Ellis playing in 1825?

(If your answers to the above two questions are the same then please answer this question)

How can William Webb Ellis have invented a game that he was already playing?

(If your answers to the two questions are different then please answer this question)

Where are the changes in the laws and in the name of the actual game as it was agreed upon by the people who were playing it? If Webb Ellis invented a game, why was there no change?

If Rugby Union was a running game when William Webb Ellis died in 1872, 49 years after he was supposed to have invented a game that nobody at the time knew he had invented, including himself, why was it possible to score any number of touch downs by running in with the ball and yet still lose the game by one kick (a goal) to nil?

If Webb Ellis invented Rugby Union, why was this invention not discussed for 72 years?

CONCLUSION – There is no other viable option than the origin of Rugby Union lying with the game of Football at Rugby School sometime between 1743 and 1812. The origin and evolution of Rugby Union can now be traced from the game Football at Rugby School circa 1783 to World Rugby, the governing body of Rugby Union today.

FOOTNOTE – One last song; please join me in singing the Queen classic……….

We are the Champions my friend
and we'll keep on writing to the end
We are the Champions
We are the Champions
No time for Folk Football or the Ellis Event
We are the Champions of the Origin.

CHAPTER 12 – ADDITIONAL INFORMATION – THE OLD RUGBEIAN SOCIETY 1897 REPORT

AIM – The aim of this chapter is to include additional information about the 1897 Old Rugbeian Society report.

We need to look more closely at the report and keep asking questions, because as far as I'm concerned it deliberately set out to misinform and there are several inconsistencies within the report that require investigation. Let's start with the letters contained within the report and begin with Thomas Hughes. To quote directly from the report:

"The late Judge Hughes, so well known as the author of "Tom Brown's School Days," writing from Uffington House, Chester, under the date of 14th March, 1895, characteristically replied as follows:

Dear Sir

Your Committee have raised an old and warmly debated question of half a century back." – ORSR011

Thomas Hughes starts his letter dated 14 March 1895 by referring to 'Your Committee'. The front cover of the report however states "Report (with appendices) of the sub-committee of the Old Rugbeian Society appointed in July 1895":

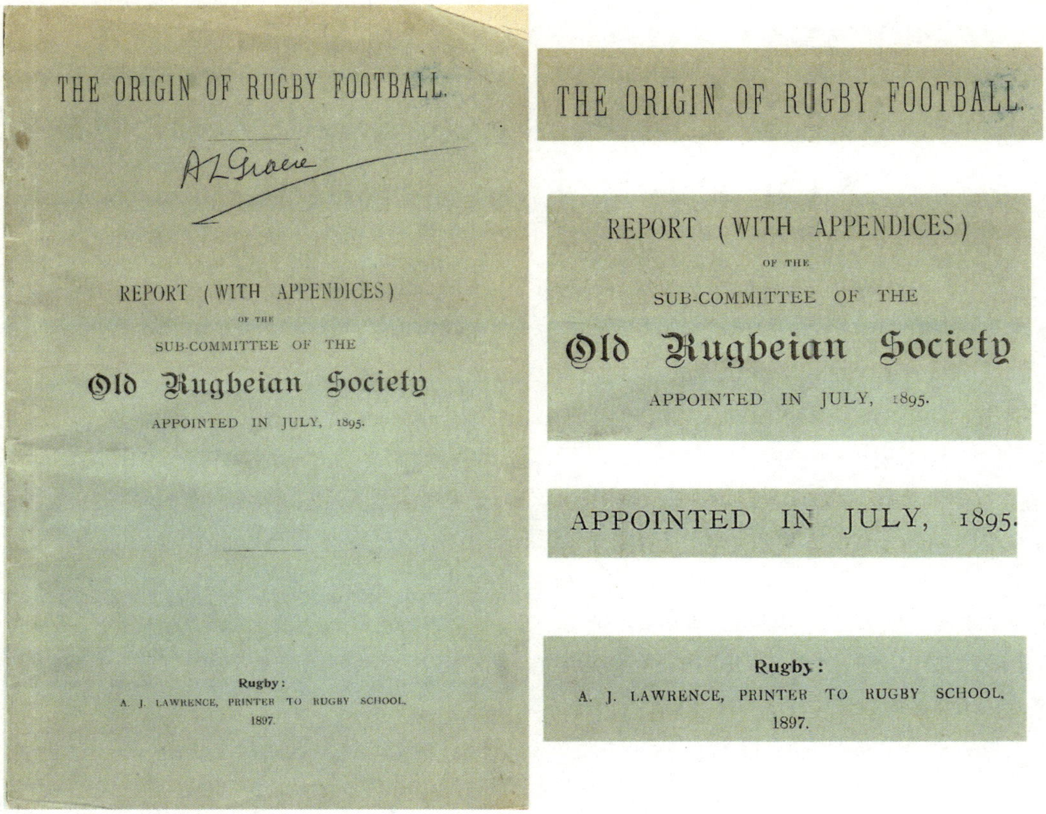
THE ORIGIN OF RUGBY FOOTBALL.

A L Gracie

REPORT (WITH APPENDICES)
OF THE
SUB-COMMITTEE OF THE
Old Rugbeian Society
APPOINTED IN JULY, 1895.

Rugby:
A. J. LAWRENCE, PRINTER TO RUGBY SCHOOL.
1897.

THE ORIGIN OF RUGBY FOOTBALL.

REPORT (WITH APPENDICES)
OF THE
SUB-COMMITTEE OF THE
Old Rugbeian Society
APPOINTED IN JULY, 1895.

APPOINTED IN JULY, 1895.

Rugby:
A. J. LAWRENCE, PRINTER TO RUGBY SCHOOL.
1897.

The front cover of the 1897 report

How can Thomas Hughes have replied to a letter from a committee that had not yet been appointed? He wrote the letter in March to a committee that wasn't convened until four months later, in July. Just in case you think that it might have been a slip of the pen, what about his second letter, dated 18 March, which ends *"All success to the Committee, of whose existence I am glad to know."* – ORSR014

It seems from the report that the majority of letters were written before the sub-committee had formed.

14 & 18 March 1895 – Thomas Hughes (died 22 March 1896)
22 March 1895 – Henry H. Gibbs (died 13 September 1907)
24 March 1895 – John R. Lyon
24 March 1895 – F. Lushington
8 May 1895 – R.W. son of Peregrine Birch
8 May 1895 – J. W. Cunningham
11 May 1895 – Henry Homer (died 16 October 1911)
13 May 1895 – Thomas Harris (died 2 August 1895)
16 May 1895 – George Chas Benn (died before publication)
23 May 1895 – Samuel Garratt
25 May 1895 – Thomas Harris (died 2nd August 1895)

6 June 1895 – R.W. son of Peregrine Birch

July 1895 – Sub-committee appointed

11 November 1895 – H.G. Allen
12 November 1895 – John Coke Fowler
25 February 1896 – F. Lushington
1 February 1897 – Alex J. Arbuthnot
17 February 1897 – F. H. Deane
4 May 1897 – Canon H. R. Nevill of Norwich

circa July 1897 – Report printed

During my research I struggled to understand how this could have been, and was also concerned about the deaths of a number of the above letter writers, including Thomas Hughes and George Chas Benn, between the date that the letter was written and the date of its publication. The most significant of these is Thomas Harris; I'll quote directly from the report:

"... in the person of the Rev. T Harris, brother of Mr E Harris the solicitor at Rugby, who have both died within the last two years. From him, through the kindness of his friend, the Rev. H. Homer, the following exceedingly interesting particulars were obtained, affording a remarkable corroboration of Mr. Bloxam's statements. We print Mr. Homer's letter first..." – ORSR019

I thought it wise to check out the original correspondence at the Rugby School library and I arrived with a list of letters from six correspondents that I'd identified as needing closer inspection.

There were no envelopes accompanying any of the letters and whilst I was expecting this and the lack of envelopes does not signify anything untoward, the sight of an envelope with a dated postmark would have been welcomed. There weren't any original enquiry letters either, which I found unusual. It would have been nice to have seen the questions asked, alongside any information that had been volunteered with the questions. The original correspondence is bound into a volume and a welcome addition to the collection is a series of letters from Morris Davies, the Old Rugbeian Society secretary to Mr H.F. Wilson, one of the compilers of the report. This series of letters was helpful in identifying why some of the responses pre-dated the formation of the sub-committee. I believe this series of letters to be important and worth recording and I have therefore included them in the following chapter. With information from these letters at hand, we are able to continue answering questions like:

WHO WROTE THE REPORT?

The sub-committee was made up of Henry Francis Wilson – barrister; Herbert Henry Child – barrister; Arthur George Guillemard – solicitor; Harry Lushington Stephen – barrister.

From the additional correspondence between Davies and Wilson it becomes apparent that H.F. Wilson was the early driving force behind the report. His first contact was with every schoolboy's hero, Thomas Hughes, who wrote what I suspect was his favourite book, 'Tom Brown's Schooldays'. The committee that Hughes refers to in his letters was probably the Old Rugbeian Society committee, which I've assumed included Wilson. Hughes' reply suggests that Wilson had approached him in an official capacity on behalf of the committee. Wilson followed a line of enquiry suggested by Hughes, but it soon dried up. This clears up the problem with the dates – Wilson started the investigations as a member of the ORS committee in March 1895.

It seems that Wilson worked alone, but then drafted a report that he forwarded to Morris Davies, the ORS secretary. In a letter dated 9 May 1895, Davies says *"I have left your draft report with Mr Benn"*. Davies had contacted Benn & Homer and the latter wrote to Thomas Harris. Davies was delighted with Harris' first letter and it seems that at that point the responsibility for the report shifted. Davies assumed seniority and relentlessly pushed Wilson to write and gain more information from Harris. In between letters dated 20 May and 30 May, it seems that Wilson received a reply from Harris that was not to Davies' liking; in the letter dated 30 May Davies pushed Wilson to contact Harris again, stressing the importance of the committee's mission:

"Dear Mr Wilson, - I wonder if Mr. Harris thoroughly understands what we are at. Did you explain to him that there was a tradition, &c. to be found in Bloxam's book, and all that we wanted was some corroboration (which we hoped he could give), of the statement that Webb-Ellis was the first to run with the ball. It is not for me to suggest what you should do, but I should again press him to say what he knows about it. He must remember our hero doing something unusual" – (see Chapter 13)

Between 4 June and 31 July, Davies, who was still holding Wilson's draft report, called a meeting of the Old Rugbeian Society at which the sub-committee was formed. Unfortunately Wilson was unable to attend and the last letter in the series between Davies and Wilson, dated 6 August, informs Wilson of the sub-committee's confidence in him *"No-one thought you faithless, I explained how it was you could not turn up, and all were satisfied"*. The letter goes on to inform Wilson that he had been elected to a vacant post on the sub-committee and then waves his singular involvement goodbye with a vote of thanks *"for all he had done in re W. Webb-Ellis."* Morris Davies also added his personal gratitude *"As an O.R. I sincerely thank you for the trouble you have taken."* The letter also informed him that *"I left your report with Guillemard"*. So on 6

August 1895 we know that a sub-committee had been formed to wrest the ownership of the report from Wilson and that the report was at that point in the hands of Arthur George Guillemard.

Arthur George Guillemard.

My opinion is that Guillemard wrote the booklet 'The Origin of Rugby Football'. He was a seasoned writer of some repute, having written chapters in Marshall's book. He had attended the school 1859–1864 while the three barristers had all been contemporaries in the early 1870s. Guillemard was older and of far greater seniority in Rugby Union circles than the other three. He was also a solicitor who was used to instructing barristers. Once the sub-committee was formed, being the senior member, he took over from Wilson as the report editor. Just to be on the safe side let's read through the text to see who is mentioned where:

H.L. Stephen – In a footnote on page four, about folk football it states that "*Mr H. L. Stephen points out that by the Highway Act, 1835…*" (ORSR004), so it can't have been H.L. Stephen writing the report.

H.H. Child – In a footnote on page eight (ORSR008) it states that H.H. Child had looked up the original 1880 Times article that Bloxam referred to in his Meteor article (we've published this to www.world-rugby-museum.com if you would like to read it), so it can't have been H.H. Child writing the report.

H.F. Wilson – He was responsible for the onerous work of writing the draft report, but as we can see from the Davies–Wilson correspondence, the report was taken out of his hands and placed into Guillemard's.

A.G. Guillemard – The first mention of A.G. Guillemard by name in the report is among the final credits. If he had had another involvement, for example in writing letters or doing research, it would have been mentioned in the text. Whilst Guillemard is only mentioned by name once, he can also be found in the report itself. If you cast your mind back to the following paragraph that mentions the Standard in 1876:

"He had previously broached the subject, as he tells us in a letter headed "Football and Athletics" to the Meteor (No 104), of October 10, 1876, by writing to the Standard (in which a discussion on the game had been taking place) to controvert the belief, expressed by one of its correspondents that the Rugby game, at present played at Rugby, was 'of great and unknown antiquity.'" – ORSR011

In which *"one of its correspondents"* just so happened to be Arthur George Guillemard. To gain a better idea of the validity of Guillemard's writing, let's hop into a taxi, 'Back to the Future' style, and have a look at the London Evening Standard chain of letters from its beginning.

All aboard for the London Evening Standard of 10 February 1876…

"FATAL FOOTBALL ACCIDENT. – An inquest was held at Manchester, on Tuesday, on the body of a young man named Ison, who died on Sunday from compression of the brain, produced by injuries sustained in a football match on Saturday. Deceased, while running after the ball, was charged by one of the opposing team and knocked down. He

had to be removed in a cab, and shortly afterwards became unconscious. The jury returned a verdict of Accidental Death, and strongly recommended that "charging," "scrimmaging," "butting," and catching by the legs should be abolished in the game of football." – LEVS18760210

This report enraged Edward B. Adams M.R.C.S., a surgeon who had had enough of dealing with football injuries. He made a call for inexperienced players to be stopped from playing football by the authorities. This letter was published on 12 February.

"FOOTBALL. TO THE EDITOR OF THE STANDARD.
SIR,–In your paper of this date I read the following melancholy statement: An inquest was held at Manchester on Tuesday, on Mr. Ison, who died on Sunday from compression of the brain, produced by injuries sustained in a football match on Saturday. Deceased while running after the ball was charged by one of the opposite team, and knocked down. Verdict of the jury in accordance with the evidence and common sense. Being acquainted with the fact, as a medical man of some 26 years standing, of broken legs, fractured clavicles, injured spines, ruptures by over exertion, necrosis of the bones of the leg from blows or kicks, fractures of the ankle joint and leg, injuries to the hip-joint, with many other serious results to the development of young men engaged in this rufflianly pastime, surely a stop should at once be exercised by those in authority over the inexperienced who indulge in such wanton ruffianism as the game of football.–I remain, yours obediently, EDWARD B. ADAMS, M.R.C.S England. Bungay, Suffolk, Feb. 10." – LEVS18760212

'Headmaster' replied and his letter was published on 16 February. In it he points out that Mr Ison lost his life playing the *"modern degenerate sport"* that is Rugby Union and not football as played at Eton, Harrow, Winchester & Westminster, which are the 'oldest, manliest and best of games'.

"FOOTBALL. TO THE EDITOR OF THE STANDARD.
SIR,–Mr. Adams has written strongly against the game of football from a medical point of view. As an old public school man and a schoolmaster, I should be very sorry to see the game – as played at Eton, Harrow, Winchester, or Westminster – forbidden by any authority. It is one of the oldest, manliest, and best of games. It is more ancient than cricket, the foremost of national sports. The game through which Mr. Ison lost his life is not football properly so called – it is the game known as the "Rugby Union," and is a modification or adaptation of the Rugby School (so called) football. Persons in authority cannot do better than discourage by all means in their power this modern degenerate sport, and promote the famous, healthy, scientific, ancient, and national game of football, as played at Harrow or by "association" clubs. The popularity of the "Rugby Union" game is of very recent date: it is due to various causes, which I have no time to discuss. I see no immediate prospect of checking it, except by the influence of a sound public opinion upon the authorities of schools, such as Rugby, Marlborough, Clifton,

and Wellington. If at these schools it were forbidden it would gradually decline.–Your obedient servant, HEADMASTER. Feb. 12." – LEVS18760216

A response to Headmaster's letter by a supporter of the Rugby Union game, the then secretary of the Rugby Football Union, Arthur George Guillemard, was published on 18 February.

"FOOTBALL. TO THE EDITOR OF THE STANDARD.
SIR,–Some of the statements of your correspondent "Headmaster" are so completely at variance with facts that I trust you will allow me space briefly to reply to his letter. Firstly, he avers that the game of football as played by Rugby Union laws is not football properly so called. What "football properly so called" is he does not explain ; the fact remains that the earliest records of football matches show clearly that the game was played according to the Rugby system–namely, that its distinguishing feature lay in running with the ball. It may also be a fact of which "Headmaster" is ignorant that Rugby School was celebrated for its football many decades before the game was even taken up by Eton, Harrow, Winchester or Westminster. The Rugby game, therefore, as compared with that played at Harrow or by association clubs can hardly be called a "modern sport," and I am happy to say that its popularity is far too wide-spread to be affected by the unfounded statements of "Headmaster." He may also be surprised to hear that the accidents resulting from Rugby football are not only less numerous in proportion to the numbers playing than those resulting from the association game, but also less numerous than those that occur at any other British sport or athletic pastime. It would be well if "Headmaster" would turn his attention to the perils of rink-skating, for more accidents have happened to rink-skaters in the past three months, than to Rugby football players in three years.
"Headmaster" is evidently unacquainted with the fact that the practices that have been complained of in the old Rugby School game have been done away with by the Rugby Union code, and much as the recent accident will be deplored by football players generally, the prestige of a game which has spread to Canada and India, Australia and New Zealand, and affords healthful exercise to some thirty thousand players in our own islands, is not likely to be seriously affected by the strictures of one or two individuals, who are not acquainted with the facts of the case in point.– Yours faithfully, ARTHUR G. GUILLEMARD, Hon. Sec. Rugby Football Union, Eltham, Feb. 16." – LEVS18760218

Guillemard makes several unfounded statements that in the 1870s could not be backed up by facts or figures and so must therefore have been fabricated. For instance, he says:

"...earliest records of football show clearly that the game was played according to the Rugby system..."

"...Rugby School was celebrated for its football many decades before the game was even taken up by Eton, Harrow, Winchester or Westminster."

"He may also be surprised to hear that the accidents resulting from Rugby football are not only less numerous in proportion to the numbers playing than those resulting from the association game, but also less numerous than those that occur at any other British sport or athletic pastime."

"It would be well if "Headmaster" would turn his attention to the perils of rink-skating, for more accidents have happened to rink-skaters in the past three months, than to Rugby football players in three years."

Public Schoolman entered the debate on the same day, 18 February, and his letter was in support of Headmaster. He was an ex-public schoolboy who witnessed a 'Rugby Rules' game where a boy's leg was broken deliberately by a large man. It's not worth printing his letter here as there is nothing else of importance in it. Our main players here are Headmaster, Guillemard and Bloxam, who has yet to join in.

Headmaster responded to Guillemard's unsupported claims in a letter printed on 21 February, asking him to supply documentary evidence to prove his point. He also challenged his statement on the proportion of accidents within the two sports (Association & Rugby), again asking for evidence. He also called into question that the Rugby Rules allowed running with the ball.

"FOOTBALL. TO THE EDITOR OF THE STANDARD.
SIR,–I am glad that so stout a champion of the Rugby game as Mr. Guillemard has replied to my letter. I maintain still, until Mr. Guillemard refers me to undoubted historical testimony assorting the contrary, that the Rugby game is not the old game, as played in England before the school of Rugby was founded. He says "Rugby School was celebrated for its football many decades of years before the game was even taken up at Eton, Harrow, Winchester or Westminster." Now, unless my memory is at fault, Rugby school has not existed "many decades of years," whereas Winchester was founded in 1385, and Eton about 50 years later. Unless Mr. Guillemard can refer us to documents showing beyond question that the game, as played on English and Scotch commons, and played too, sometimes by women, was not adopted at the ancient public schools, or any football played there, until the comparatively modern school of Rugby invented their game, he will hardly establish his point in the minds of your readers.
I define football to be a game in which the ball is propelled by the feet towards a certain goal, and where the hands are used as little as possible. I refuse to believe, against the evidence of my senses, against the testimony of medical men, against the corroborative opinions of competent and impartial persons whom I have consulted, that the Association game causes more serious accidents than the Rugby Union. Upon this we want statistics, not assertions on either side.

It has been for years known to me that certain objectionable practices in the old Rugby game have been repealed in the new Rugby Union code of rules; but, au contraire, an old Rugbeian informs me that 25 years ago, or less, no player at Rugby could take the ball into his hands unless it were bounding, and that "passing on" from one to another was forbidden. He adds that in his opinion these practices are most objectionable. Many persons are at a loss to conceive what can be the great popularity of this game. When I watch it occasionally, about two thirds of the time is taken up in scrimmages; a drearier sight it is hard to imagine. I have made it my business to discover why so many people of the lower orders look on at it in our public parks, and their remarks have conclusively proved to me that what they most enjoy is not a clever kick but an ugly fall. It appeals, I fear, to the ruder and more cruel instincts of human nature among these uneducated or half-uneducated people. One of the best of our Rugby "half-backs" admitted the other day, with great frankness, that there was little fun in the game for those whose played "up."
Surely a game worth preserving should spread its excitement, and interest and skill over more than a small fraction of the combatants. The true and manly game of football is a sport wholly distinct from the Rugby hand ball. One of our new boys put it very well the other day, when he asked a master whether we "played Rugby or football at our school."

Sir, I apologise for making my remarks so long; but for the youth and future men of England this is a very important subject. My opinions have not been hastily formed; they are the same as they were when I was at Winchester more than 20 years ago–namely, that the Rugby Union game is unmanly, unscientific, too rough for most boys, too dangerous for all men; that it is no more to be compared to true football than battledore and shuttle-cock to tennis, or trap bat to cricket; that its popularity is on all grounds to be deplored, and greatly on this–that very few but the sons of gentlemen, for example, at Rugby, Marlborough, or the Universities, can indulge in it without a lowering effect on their disposition, and an ungentle influence on their lives.–Your obedient servant, HEADMASTER, London, Feb. 18." – LEVS18760221

In a letter published on 24 February, Guillemard admits to his lack of statistics but pushes the folk football games as being the origin of Rugby Union.

"FOOTBALL. TO THE EDITOR OF THE STANDARD.
SIR,–"Headmaster" seems anxious to obtain more information regarding the early history of football than can be gleaned from a whole library of cyclopædias. It is not very difficult to go back to the Roman Harpastum, about which Pollux says, "The players divided themselves into two bands, and at the two ends, behind the places where the players were stationed, there were two lines (goal lines), beyond which they tried to carry the ball–a feat that could not be accomplished without pushing one another backwards and forwards." As Mr. Alcock remarks in his "Football, our Winter Game," it does not show any great credulity to assume that this rough sport was introduced into

Britain by the Romans, and there is good reason to believe that it was the parent of English Football. At any rate there were goals and two sides of players who had to drive the ball from the end to end of a strip of ground.
Probably the earliest record of a football match in Great Britain is that given by Sir T. Morton Eden, in his "Statistical Account of Scotland," with reference to the great annual game at the Cross of Scone, played by the bachelors and married men of the parish on Shrove Tuesday. "The game was this–he who at any time got the ball into his hands ran with it till he was overtaken by a player of the opposite party, and then if he could shake himself loose from those who were holding him, he ran on; if not, he threw the ball from him, unless it was wrested from him by one of the other party; but no person was allowed to kick it." The goals were a river at one end of the ground and a hole on the moor at the other. And as to football as played in the earliest times on our village commons, the players were at liberty to carry the ball or kick it as they pleased. So that if "Headmaster" wishes to trace the game back to the fountain head I may repeat that "the earliest records of football matches show clearly that the game was played according to the Rugby system–namely, that its distinguishing feature lay in running with the ball."

With football, as with cricket, I think there can be little doubt that until a comparatively recent period rules, if, indeed, as regards football, any at all existed, were of the very crudest description. And although I admit the older standing of Eton and Winchester, and that an Etonian and Wykhamist may have kicked a football before ever a Rugbeian was born, still, on the other hand, the public will agree that first of all schools, Rugby made herself a name by her football rules. And I may here be allowed to deprecate "Headmaster's" statement that "Rugby School has not existed many decades of years:" it was founded by a good old grocer, one Lawrence Sherriffe, in 1573, and, as it has celebrated its tercentenary, can hardly be termed "a comparatively modern school." I am glad to ascertain "Headmaster's" definition of football, especially as it exactly coincides with my expectations. He is of opinion that the hands should be brought into play as little as possible: in fact, that carrying the ball is not football. This is of all arguments the most hackneyed, and has been met twenty times in as many different journals. In the earliest times was a name fixed upon and then a game established in accordance with it? Why should the name exercise an arbitrary authority over the rules, and if (as is the case) the large majority of football players consider the game improved by carrying, why should the fact that nothing relating to it can be inferred from the name prevent their adoption of the practice? Like "Headmaster's" as regards the Association rules, I have no detailed statistics as to accidents at the Rugby game, but can only say that, as far as I can remember, only three serious accidents occurred in the matches in which I myself took part during fourteen football seasons at Rugby and round London, and I may reiterate that so small a proportion of accidents would not have occurred at any other English out-door pastime. And, finally, "Headmaster's" isolated instances of players who are dissatisfied with the Rugby game prove nothing whatever, when even an inveterate opponent like himself cannot help admitting its great and general popularity. The crack Rugby half back who thought there was very little fun in playing forward is a mere counterpart of the crack bowler in the eleven who cannot see much pleasure in fielding at short leg. Two out of three football players are forward players, so surely the game has attractions for more than a small fraction of the combatants. If "Headmaster" is of opinion that a drearier sight than Rugby football match it is hard to imagine, by all means let him feast his eyes on an Association game: but when he proceeds to stigmatise the favourite English winter game as "unmanly and unscientific," and having a lowering effect on the disposition and an ungentle influence on the lives of many players, he descends to a crushing condemnation of a healthful sport, which it would be absurd for me to criticise, and in which he will be supported by no single person who has had any practical experience of Rugby football.–Yours faithfully, ARTHUR G. GUILLEMARD. Hon. Sec. Rugby Football Union. Eltham, Feb. 22." – LEVS18760224

Enter Matthew Holbeche Bloxam, corresponding with the Standard *"to controvert the belief by one of its correspondents"* (as phrased by the ORS Report – OSRS011) and to set the record straight with regards to the practice of 'running with the ball'. This letter was published on 26 February 1876.

"FOOTBALL. TO THE EDITOR OF THE STANDARD.
SIR,–Permit an old Rugbeian, at school under the headmastership of Dr. Wooll, who resigned that office in the summer of 1828, to say a few words on the point in controversy in the present Rugby game. The running with the ball in one's hands is of no great antiquity as regards Rugby, it has there originated within the last half-century. It was not so during Dr. Wooll's mastership. When a boy had caught the ball in his hands he was not allowed to run forwards with it, but marking with the heel of his foot the spot where he had caught it, he was permitted without molestation to go back on his own side as far as he chose, the opposite side not being allowed to cross the point where the ball had been caught. He who had caught the ball might then either punt it, or place it on the ground and kick it, or allow some one else on his side to kick it so placed; but directly the ball touched the ground, the opposite side might rush forward and contend. Such was the rule of the game at Rugby School fifty years ago. MATTHEW HOLBECHE BLOXAM, at Rugby School from 1813 to 1821, and ever since a resident at Rugby. Feb. 24." – LEVS18760226

And so the series of letters to the London Evening Standard ended with Guillemard being a driving force for folk football being the origin of Rugby Union – *"So that if "Headmaster" wishes to trace the game back to the fountain head I may repeat that "the earliest records of football matches show clearly that the game was played according to the Rugby system – namely, that its distinguishing features lay in running with the ball."*

With respect to the 1897 'Origin of Rugby Football' report, we can assume that after Wilson was relieved of the duty of writing it, the responsibility then passed to Arthur G Guillemard because of his service to the Rugby Football Union, his authorship of Marshall's chapters, his writing of letters to the newspapers and his senior position within the Rugby fraternity. The Davies–Wilson letters have however thrown up another question. Was Morris Davies secretly the leader and the real driving force behind 'the plaque in the wall gang'? Did he initially detail Wilson to compile the report and when he became dissatisfied with Wilson's handling of Thomas Harris, organise the sub-committee takeover, making sure that the report passed into the hands of his old and trusted friend Arthur Guillemard? It seems that the plaque in the wall was his idea, put forward in a letter dated 6 August 1895. This was two years before the investigation was concluded and the report was published. Davies had already decided its outcome: Webb Ellis was a hero and he already knew where the 'granite slab' was to be placed.

6 August 1895 – *"I would again suggest that we place a handsome granite slab (with inscription, of course) in the Headmaster's wall, exactly opposite the centre of the school goal, to commemorate our hero's invention. Of course you can do what you like, but I believe that idea is as sensible as any. Yours sincerely, MORRIS DAVIES." (see chapter 13)*

To our original four members of the 'plaque in the wall gang' – Wilson, Child, Stephen and Guillemard – we must now add Morris Davies. These five Old Rugbeians, Davies in particular, are guilty of having perverted the course of history. When they named Webb Ellis as the inventor of Rugby Union and laid the plaque in the headmaster's wall, the true originators of the sport, the pupils who decided that the goal was above the crossbar missed out, it was they who deserve the acclaim that Webb Ellis received. It is they who are the true inventors of Rugby Union and they deserve to be recognized as such.

SUMMARY – If the report was intended to be an unbiased review of the origin of Rugby Football, it had no chance. The report had one purpose and that was to place the origin of Rugby Football at Rugby School. Two years before its publication, Morris Davies, the secretary of the ORS, had already decided that Webb Ellis was a hero and that a plaque saying so should be cemented into the headmaster's wall at Rugby School. In forming a sub-committee of the ORS, Davies used his position of authority to wrest the report from its author H.F. Wilson and he handed it to his old friend Arthur George Guillemard. It is most likely that Guillemard wrote the report; he is mentioned in it, but not named. As can be seen from the series of letters he wrote to the London Standard, he has previously fabricated information to support his theories. Matthew Bloxam ended the series of letters with his recollection of how the game was played, stating that running with the ball was a modern invention.

CONCLUSION – The ORS report titled 'Origin of Rugby Football' has altered the true history of the sport of Rugby Union.

FOOTNOTE – Think back to the beginning of the chain of Standard letters; in your mind, when you read that Ison had been removed in a cab, did you picture him in a black London taxi like the one that we went 'back to the future' in? If you did, you should know that they didn't exist in Manchester in 1876 – the first car didn't appear until 1886. A cab in those days was drawn by horses. That was my little 'thought suggestion' trick, and speaking of tricks, did you believe me when I said that the answer to our sumspeed game was really 5919? Because the answer is really 5929.

Following in the footsteps of the Old Rugbeian Society Report, Jenny Macrory's book 'Running With the Ball – the Birth of Rugby Football' did exactly the same thing as the 1897 publication, just 94 years later. The title tells you that running with the ball was the birth of rugby football and that the 'plaque in the wall gang' confirmed the findings of Bloxam, the *'honest antiquarian'*. She omitted the date that the committee was appointed (in July 1895) but included the letters written in March prior to this. She also avoided the 1824 and 1825 inconsistencies in Bloxam's mentions of Ellis.

I bet that you have now checked, with a calculator of course, that 77 x 77 is 5929. If you hadn't checked before now then I'm still the winner, if you had then congratulations, you beat me at sumspeed. If you knew automatically that 5929 was the correct answer without checking anything then you are a natural and you need to enter the Intergalactic Sumspeed Championships being held on Mars in the year 5929. That's our 5929, not the Martian year 5929, which has already been and gone.

CHAPTER 13 – CORRESPONDENCE FROM DAVIES TO WILSON

TROY HOUSE, RUGBY. *May 7th*, 1895.

DEAR MR. WILSON,

I called on Mr. George Benn on Sunday. He recollects Mrs. Ellis quite well, and also the name of our hero, but does not remember ever having seen him. He entered the School in 1830, only 7 years after 'the Event' and vividly remembers what the Football was then like.

He tells me that there were no backs or half-backs, but the bigger boys used to stand back and run with the ball, &c. Before he left, Theodore Walrond introduced a system of backs and half-backs and after leaving Oxford sent down a set of draft Rules on approval. Mr. Benn is convinced that Theodore Walrond perfected the game and deserves the credit.

I saw Child yesterday and he thinks we should commit Mr. Benn's recollections to writing–but what if they do not agree with Tom Hughes's? Mr. Benn would like to see what the latter wrote. Have you a copy of such letter?

Mr. Benn says there are but three Houses now that existed in Webb-Ellis's time–the School House (just as it is), our old House (Whitelaw's) and Payne Smith's. He remembers all the others being built–as *new* ventures.

I have got the fellows in the School House and Bowden Smith's to look up their records and will let you know what they find. The records of Whitelaw's have been destroyed by fire you say. Would it not be wise to ask S. H. Walrond to look up his father's papers? He may find some record of the introduction of the game–at any rate he may find the original Rules referred to by Mr. Benn; his address is 65, Lancaster Gate.

What about Lord Bangor? Could he not give you some assistance? Theodore Walrond's brother tells me he was here about Mr. Benn's time.

You probably know that the badges worn on the football caps and jerseys were invented by General Henry Hope Crealock, C.B., and have, I believe, never been altered. He entered the School in 1844.

Kindly let me know what I can do to help you.

Yours very truly,

MORRIS DAVIES.

TROY HOUSE, RUGBY. *May 9th*, 1895.

DEAR MR. WILSON,

I have left your Draft Report with Mr. Benn who will commit to paper his reminiscences.

He advises our writing to Sir W. Cunliffe Brookes, Bart., who was a prominent footballer in his day.

Mr. Lawrence recommends your writing to Mr. Samuel Garratt, who entered in 1831, and lives at

Rocheberie,
Blackwater Road,
Eastbourne.

and says that one James Voile, at one time owner of Billington's shop, but now an inmate of some Free-Masons' Institution was until lately alive, if he is not so now. Would it be of any use our writing to him? He entered the School in 1823.

I have examined Mr. Lawrence's ledgers, and cannot find an entry for printing Football Rules earlier than Oct. 1847, when 50 copies were printed for the Rev. T. L. Bloxam, brother of Matthew Bloxam.

If there are any other such entries for printing Rules they could only be found by asking Mr. Clarke, Bookseller, Leicester.

Who succeeded Crossley,
" " Combe,
" " Rowell.

(Rowell was the School printer in 1823 and 1824.) He may have some such entry.

Yours very truly,

MORRIS DAVIES.

TROY HOUSE, RUGBY, *May* 18, 1895.

DEAR MR. WILSON,

I herewith send you what I consider a very valuable letter from

The Rev. Thos. Harris,
The Rectory,
Swerford,
Enstone.

He entered the School in 1819 and left in 1828.

From it I gather that he unconsciously supports Mr. Bloxam's tradition, for on page 2 he says that our hero "was generally regarded as inclined to take unfair advantages at football," which is just what Bloxam states. Mr. Bloxam, as you know, does not maintain that after Ellis's exploit in 1823 the practice of "running with the ball," as he did, was adopted. On the contrary, he says that it remained in abeyance until Arnold's time (1828).

It is just possible that "running with the ball" was legalized between the time in 1828, when Harris left, and 1830, when Mr. G. C. Benn came.

I have seen the latter this morning. He will commit his reminiscences to writing by to-night, and I will send them to you by to-morrow's post.

As I leave early to-morrow morning, I think it better to send you the letter at once, so that you may administer fresh interrogatories to the Rev. T. Harris if you think it necessary.

Yours very truly,

MORRIS DAVIES.

TROY HOUSE, RUGBY, *May 20th*, 1895.

DEAR MR. WILSON,

Although, when we remember Mr. Thomas Harris's great age, there is no time to be lost if we want to clear up through him, the Webb-Ellis peculiarities of play, I think you should know that his younger brother, Edmund, the Rugby solicitor, died quite suddenly on Friday last. This may prevent his replying at once to any questions you may put to him.

In order to make recent Rugbeians buy your pamphlet, what do you say for or against printing the names of the School 'Fifteens' since their formation (and the 'Twenties' also, for the matter of that), and any other information connected with the game that we may hit upon? I would supply you with the names. Mr. Benn–whom I thanked *for you* yesterday–is very anxious you should write to the brothers Arbuthnot. He looks upon them as the greatest authorities bar "Jim Mackie," who appears to have been head and shoulders ahead of any one. But of course you can do as you like. Please let me know if you succeed in getting from Mr. Harris the confirmation of Bloxam's statement. I hope most sincerely you will.

Yours very truly,

MORRIS DAVIES.

TROY HOUSE, RUGBY. *May 30th*, 1895.

DEAR MR. WILSON,

I wonder if Mr. Harris thoroughly understands what we are at. Did you explain to him that there was a tradition, &c. to be found in Bloxam's book, and all that we wanted was some corroboration (which we hoped he could give), of the statement that Webb-Ellis was first to run with the ball.

It is not for me to suggest what you should do, but I should again press him to say what he knows about it. He must remember our hero doing something unusual.

I enclose a card kindly forwarded me by Mr. Hyde Harrison–who keeps a Preparatory School at Dunchurch - and a cutting from the *Field* ; he is not sure of the year, but Farwell, Q.C. (whom you probably know) was playing I see, and could supply the exact date. Is it worth printing in the book?

The Boys think that a list of all Twenties and Fifteens would be interesting, and lead to the sale of the book. I was *astonished* to find that the Head of the XV. keeps no record of the fellows who play with him. But I can get the names for you. I hope yet to find that there is a map on the Conveyance of the Close to the Governing Body in 1749.

Yours very truly,

MORRIS DAVIES.

TROY HOUSE, RUGBY, *June* 4, 1895.

DEAR MR. WILSON,

Having just received the enclosed card (which answers your queries) I at once return Mr. Harris' valuable letter.

I showed it to Mr. Benn, who again said "I hope Mr. Wilson has written to the Arbuthnots." He evidently considers them to have been something out of the common as football players. He will never rest satisfied until he hears from me that you have written.

Shall I get out for you the names of all "Twenties" and "Fifteens" to date?

I am led to suppose that there was no map on the conveyance of the Close to the Governing Body.

Yours sincerely,

MORRIS DAVIES.

TROY HOUSE, RUGBY. *Aug. 6th*, 1895.

DEAR MR. WILSON,

No one thought you faithless. I explained how it was you could not turn up, and all were satisfied.

As you were not present, we refrained from reading the report, but resolved that the matter should be left in your, Child's, Stephen's, and Guillemard's hands, to deal with as you might determine.

You were elected to one of the vacancies on the Committee and you also received a vote of thanks for all you had done in *re* W. Webb-Ellis.

I left your report with Guillemard who promised to call on you ; in your hands it may be safely left. As an O.R. I sincerely thank you for the trouble you have taken.

I would again suggest that we place a handsome granite slab (with inscription, of course) in the Headmaster's wall, exactly opposite the *centre* of the School goal, to commemorate our hero's invention. Of course you can do what you like, but I believe that idea is as sensible as any.

Yours sincerely,

MORRIS DAVIES.

CHAPTER 14 – RICHARDS RULES ON THE ORIGIN & EVOLUTION OF A SPORT

I hope that you've enjoyed this book. For me it's been an immense learning process. Not just about the history of Rugby Union, but also about the make-up of games and sports, and about myself. I've learnt a lot about the process of thinking and how to harness my subconscious; although setting it all down on paper has been a whole other challenge. But what of my journey – the one that started at the dentist? I now understand the origin of Rugby Union and so that journey has reached its destination. I do however feel as though I need to go further, that there is more to come. So what is next for me? Do I now chronicle the rest of the history of Rugby Union as I had originally intended, or do I change tack and analyse the origins of more sports? I prefer the latter option, which is why I've titled this book Volume One; to me that sounds a far more interesting challenge. With this in mind, based on the findings in this book, I feel confident enough to write the...........................

Richards Rules on the Origin & Evolution of a Sport

Version 1 – November 2016

THE ORIGIN OF A SPORT

The ORIGIN of a GAME or SPORT is the point in time at which a game/sport becomes identifiable as a single entity. From that point onwards it must have an evolutionary path, drawn either theoretically or through the provision of evidence, to the modern day version of the sport to be considered the origin.

GAME – A game is a contest of luck and/or mental or physical skill between two or more parties under a common set of rules with the aim of determining a desired outcome or winner.

SPORT – A sport is a contest between two or more parties of physical skill, strength, speed, endurance, ability or physical artistic impression undertaken within a common set of rules set by a governing body with the aim of determining a desired outcome or winner.

Games and sports originate from one of two methods:

1. ORIGIN BY BIRTH – Where a game/sport begins through a series of circumstances containing the six ingredients of location, personnel, equipment (optional), actions, aims and rules, which develop into a game/sport.

2. ORIGIN BY CREATION – There are three known types of origin by creation:

CREATION BY SEPARATION – Where a game/sport evolves through separation from another game/sport that continues in its own right as a parent game/sport (e.g. Rugby Union and Rugby League).

CREATION BY DESIGN – A game/sport that is designed by a person or group of people prior to the first contest taking place (it may be based on contributory games/sports, e.g. Triathlon, or be an entirely new game/sport).

CREATION BY MODEL – Where a game/sport begins by modelling itself on another sport but then follows its own line of evolution (e.g. Football at Rugby School and Football at Eton School).

The terminology for related sports should be as follows:

Parent game/sport – the game/sport from which another game/sport has derived

Descendant game/sport – a game/sport that has evolved from another game/sport

Ancestor game/sport – a game/sport in the direct lineage of the game/sport in question.

Contributory game/sport – a game/sport that is not considered to be the parent sport but has either directly or indirectly influenced another game/sport.

THE 6 INGREDIENTS OF A GAME OR A SPORT

LOCATION – This is where the game or sport will take place; a location can include fixed objects such as buildings, trees and other unavoidable factors such as water. Among others a location could be a field (cricket, soccer, *etc.*), court (tennis, basketball, *etc.*), water (swimming, diving, yachting, *etc.*), mountain (skiing, bobsleigh, orienteering, *etc.*) or road (running, cycling, *etc.*). Other permanent fixtures of a game/sport that must be present at the location and that aren't supposed to move, or are meant to be avoided during play, are also included in this ingredient – e.g. a tennis net, rugby posts, soccer goals or slalom poles.

PERSONNEL – The people and/or animals that are at the location and that are going to play and/or judge the game/sport. This includes a player's dress and equipment worn or used that is necessary to take part in a game/sport. Things like boxing gloves, swimming goggles, running shoes, skis, ski poles or tennis, badminton and squash racquets can all be considered under 'personnel'.

EQUIPMENT – The moveable objects; things that are controlled by the players and are used during the game/sport. These may already be at the location or can be brought by the personnel. Equipment, however, is not a necessity and a game/sport can take place without this component. Examples of equipment are balls, arrows, shuttlecocks, darts, pucks, javelins, discus, *etc.*, *i.e.* items that require an action to be exerted upon them in order to make them a part of the game/sport.

ACTIONS – There needs to be movement or interaction between the above three or the first two. This can include all types of movement, such as running, kicking, hitting, paddling, throwing, dancing, driving, shooting, jumping, dribbling with a ball, *etc.*

AIMS – The above actions need to be channelled into aims. There are two types of aims: 'action aims', where there are aims to the actions – e.g. passing a ball to a player in a better position, hitting a shuttlecock to put your opponent in a difficult position, bowling a ball to try and get your opponent out, scoring a goal, forcing an error, hitting a winner, running the fastest, avoiding poles, *etc.* There must also be 'objective aims' – e.g. to score more goals than the other team, to score more points, to reach a points target first, to give the best artistic impression, to jump further than anyone else, to reach the finish line first, *etc.*

RULES – A set of rules needs to be created in order to determine how the actions and aims define the contest – e.g. you can't pass forward, if you hit a pole you lose points, the first to the finish line is the winner, you mustn't punch an opponent, the game ends after 60 minutes, *etc.*

THE EVOLUTION OF A GAME OR A SPORT

A game/sport will evolve through changes in rules or laws, usually to:

1. Solve any problems that occur.

2. Take opportunities to enhance a game/sport.

When outlining the status of a game or sport in relation to its evolution, the following terminology should apply:

Steps 1-5 – PLAY – A combination of location, personnel, equipment, actions and aims without a set of rules to define a contest can be regarded as play.

Step 6 – GAME – Play becomes a game when a rule or a set of verbal rules is added to the five ingredients (equipment optional) to define the contest.

Step 7 – ORGANISED GAME – A game can be considered to be organised if a set of written rules exist under which the game is played.

Step 8 – SPORT – A game becomes a sport when a body consisting of a variety of unconnected parties that are linked only by the game played are joined together to form a governing body for the game, with a view to organising that game.

Step 9 – NATIONAL SPORT – A sport becomes national when it has a governing body that covers all regions of a particular country.

Step 10 – INTERNATIONAL SPORT – When a sport has a governing body consisting of a variety of national governing bodies that are joined together to form a governing body for the game it becomes an international sport.

RULES/LAWS

A game or sport has to have a set of rules or laws to define the contest. These rules can be split into the following categories:

KNOWLEDGE – Identifying the location, personnel and equipment to be used in the game. Explaining the terminology used in the set of rules/laws and the way in which a game is to be played.

ACTION – Directing an action that is to take place during the game.

AIM – Identifying the aim or object of a game – e.g. to score goals, first across the line, most points, best artistic impression, *etc.*

RESTRICTION – Creating boundaries for the actions, general play or other possible problems that may occur in a game.

Rules or laws can also be a combination of any of the above.

RECORDING & DECIDING ON THE ORIGIN OF A SPORT

ACCEPTABLE THEORIST – Someone who is in a position to have a theory that can be accepted or believed through means of control, for example a sport's governing body (e.g. World Rugby), an educational establishment or through information generation, for example through books, media outlets, TV, newspapers, websites, *etc.*

EARLIEST AGREED ORIGIN – The earliest point in time where it is accepted by all acceptable theorists that a game or sport exists.

EARLIEST POSSIBLE ORIGIN – The earliest point in time at which an acceptable theorist believes that a game originated.

NOTES ON THE ORIGIN – If factual evidence for the origin of a sport does not exist and there are several theoretical versions, then the probability of each possible origin theory should be decided upon by a group of 'origin specialists' who are neutral and who have no connection to an organisation within that sport. The origin specialists may if necessary seek the advice of specialists within the sport in order to examine the possibilities offered.

The above set of rules has only been checked against game-related sports. Other types of sports, such as target sports, fighting sports, physical artistic impression sports and racing sports, may have different sets of rules or criteria that apply to their origin and evolution. As with the rules and laws of games and sports, these rules may and will most likely change as more information becomes available. They are subject to the evolutionary process and are open for debate and discussion. The above rules and any future versions can be found on the below website.

www.origin-of-sport.com

CHAPTER 15 – THE FUTURE

PART ONE – THE HISTORY OF RUGBY UNION

"Whether or not rugby union is inimical to the arts, it has been careless with its history. It has enshrined its dubious myth of foundation in naming it's World Cup trophy after William Webb Ellis." – HRGH021

The above quote is from Huw Richards' 'A Game for Hooligans – The History of Rugby Union' published in 2006. I'm not so sure that the game has been careless with its history; I think it was more of a case of being misled by 'the plaque in the wall gang'. The 1897 report was one of sport's greatest confidence tricks, the irony being that it was the boys of Rugby School prior to Webb Ellis who were the actual founders of the game. They have ultimately been the big losers in the chronicling of the game.

I will be sending a copy of this book free of charge to the governing body, World Rugby. The ball is then in their hands. Will they run with it or kick for goal? I challenge World Rugby to put right its history and attribute its origin to the boys of Rugby School who invented their game. I doubt that anyone within the organisation will bother though, seeing as though they've stuck with Webb Ellis for 120 years. This might just wind up as another 'revisionist theory' to be swept under their extremely lumpy carpet. But at least we've tried and at least we now understand about the origin of Rugby Union, and when somebody tries to feed us rugby's historical bollocks in the future, we can put them straight.

PART 2 - THE FUTURE OF THE SPORT OF RUGBY UNION

So what of the future of the sport? It is my opinion that the sport of Rugby Union is heading in the direction of American Football. The more the world's governing body pushes the sport towards a running contact game, the more injuries will occur, the less people will take it up, the less parents will encourage their children to play and the more elitist the sport will become. At present a Rugby Union match is more of a gladiatorial contest than a sport of skill and strategy. In the 1880 article to which Bloxam replied, according to the author there were twice as many Rugby Union players as there were Association football players. In a 2012–13 Sport England survey, there were 11 times more Association football players (1.94 million) in England than Rugby Union players (166,400). If you took the numbers worldwide, including countries like Brazil, Spain and Germany, there would be a far greater proportion, again weighing towards the association game. Association football has understood from day one how to build its sport into the most popular worldwide, while Rugby Union has pushed the contact game to the fore and lost thousands of players as a result.

My own case study: Dai Richards – yes that's me. I started refereeing at 17 because I didn't have the confidence to play. One day a committee man talked me into playing and he refereed instead. I enjoyed the game, joined my local youth team, trained hard, worked hard on the tackle bags and on my skills. I played No. 10 (outside half, fly half, first five eighth) and in my second season, on a wet, windy afternoon, a No. 8 picked the ball off the scrum and ran straight at me. I dipped my shoulder as I'd learnt with the tackle bags and the No. 8 kept moving forward and my shoulder went with him. It dislocated and the only positive side was that we won the game 6–3, my two goals (a penalty and drop goal) to a single penalty goal. I came back from injury too early and within six months my shoulder popped again and again. I lasted another half season and when I retired from rugby at the age of 21 my shoulder was (and still is) a wreck. The next season I took an easy option and played soccer and had another two seasons at that sport before moving on to athletics and triathlon for the next 30 years. During competition in both of those sports I never once had a traumatic injury like the one I had in rugby.

If the sport continues in its current vein then I'd anticipate that in the next ten years there will be at least one death on the field or death caused by an injury received while a top class match is being watched by millions on live TV. If this happens the sport will lose thousands of players overnight. I'm not a doctor, but then again you don't need to be a doctor to see the damage that is being caused by the immense collisions in the current methods of play. The next step is protective wear for everyone. Helmets, shoulder pads and masses of padding, just like American Football. The answer is to accept that the sport is and always has been a kicking one. Running, like scrummaging and line outs, and passing the ball can be part of the sport, but it's at its best and safest in open play. Think back to what was voted as the try of the last century – Philippe St Andre's against England in 1991. There was Jonathan Webb's wayward kick and then the move that ended in the try that itself included two kicks. So that was three kicks in total for the greatest try of the century. And what about Gareth Edwards' try for the Barbarians against the All Blacks in 1973? That all came from a Bryan Williams kick downfield that was fielded by Phil Bennett. Kicks that remain in play and create space allow players the room to run with the ball. Consider the following as an immediate improvement in the sport:

Mike Brown, the England full back, has just scored a try in the corner and I have to spend 20-30 seconds watching players hug and kiss and congratulate Mike, then upwards of a minute watching Owen Farrell take a kick, with his look at the posts, look at the ball, look at the posts, look at the ball, step backwards and approach to the ball. It's like watching paint dry. Farrell's a good kicker but I refuse to watch his endless preparations.

How about this for a change in the rules relating to the goal/conversion after a try:

Goal from a place kick after a try = 1 point

Goal from a drop kick after a try = 2 points

Goal from a drop kick after a try within 30 seconds of the ball being touched down = 3 points

Goal from a drop kick after a try from outside the 22 metre line within 30 seconds of the ball being touched down, where the ball must be kicked from behind the goal line to the player kicking the conversion = 4 points

There would be rules and regulations to sort out with the retiring opposing team but think of what just happened. We speeded up the game, introduced additional tactics and increased the possible accumulative value of scoring a try, all by introducing more kicking into the game.

Rugby League has recently introduced the 40–20 rule to encourage tactical kicking and Rugby Union could do the same. What about if you kick the ball from your own half and if it goes into touch within 22 metres of you opponent's goal line, then the attacking team get the throw in. An additional provision to this rule would be that the ball has to bounce outside of the 15 metre (end of the line out) line before going into touch. This would encourage diagonal kicks with the ball bouncing further infield, which would allow defending players a greater chance of picking up the ball and counter-attacking. Running in broken play is the key to increasing the popularity of the sport for spectators and the enjoyment of the game for the players. The sight of Shane Williams in full flight, side stepping and swerving, is what makes the game of rugby a spectator sport, not watching forwards pick and drive for a metre at a time for 20 phases. Not forgetting that less contact means fewer injuries.

Rugby Union currently has a 'collision culture' and if the sport is to survive as a mass participation sport then it must move away from this.

ACKNOWLEDGEMENTS

There are several people who I would like to thank for their help, principally my wife Hayley who has supported me throughout the writing of this book. My initial readers, Ralph Holland, Nick Thomas, Alan Evans & 'Charlie' Cokely of paper clip olympic fame for their thoughts. The archivists of Eton College (including James Harrison) and Rusty Maclean of Rugby School without whom I would have been lost. Those I've bounced opinions off, Jackie Hannem Bowen, Heather Pierce, John Jones, Mark Walker & Graham Williams. The experts I've consulted, Adam Brand (handwriting) and John Griffiths for his constructive criticism and initial editing skills. My proof readers, Neilson Kite, Alan Hughes & Lindsay Devereux.

I would like to give a massive thank you to my daughter Dr Victoria Richards (Chapter 6) for the final edit of my manuscript and for listening to my non-stop chatter about the book during its writing.

To all those who have helped me or joined me as friend or foe in my sporting endeavours, you've all helped in the learning process. To those that have supported me in my sports, in particular Col Mervyn Lloyd & Barrie Smith of the 4th Battalion, Royal Regiment of Wales, the late great Maurice Levenson, aka Schmoo of Schmoo's Cycles. To all my Kiwi friends: Geoff and Barbara Miller, Steve Harvey, Jo Wing, Ken Hughey, Alastair McLean & Jayne Mossman for putting up with me on my trips to New Zealand 1992-2003.

Thnak you to John Sullivan, my ex-manager at Baglan Boys Club (Association football) 2nd team, I keep waiting to bump into him to thank him for the fantastic two seasons I had under his leadership. He was a wonderful inspiration and a great role model to us youngsters. His last word before we ran out onto the pitch was always 'ENJOY' and I believe that's something we all need to do when we play sport. ENJOY!

THANK YOU

If I've left anyone out please accept my apologies, you know how bad my memory is. I have not done this intentionally; please let me know and I will acknowledge you in any subsequent editions.

Thank you reader for joining me in this journey. I hope you've enjoyed the book, but more than that I hope you've learnt something and I hope that you too now understand about the origin of a game and a sport and in particular the sport of Rugby Union and if you see me in the street please call me 'Dai Understanding', because that's who I am.

And finally, one last song from the Sound of Music as we close the cover of the book.

So-long, farewell, auf wiedersehen, goodbye....................

.... I've read the book, now it is time to fly.

GOOOOOOOOOOOOOOOOODBYYYYYYYYYYEEEEEEEEEEEEE